How to Read the Akashic Records

ALSO BY LINDA HOWE

The Heart of the Akashic Records Revealed

Healing Through the Akashic Records

Discover Your Soul's Path Through the Akashic Records

Akashic Manifesting

100+ Questions & Answers About the Akashic Records

How to Read the Akashic Records

ACCESSING THE ARCHIVE OF
THE SOUL AND ITS JOURNEY:
REVISED AND UPDATED

Linda Howe

ST. MARTIN'S
ESSENTIALS
NEW YORK

Published in the United States by St. Martin's Essentials, an imprint of St. Martin's Publishing Group

EU Representative: Macmillan Publishers Ireland Ltd, 1st Floor, The Liffey Trust Centre, 117–126 Sheriff Street Upper, Dublin 1, D01 YC43

How to Read the Akashic Records—Revised and Updated. Copyright © 2026 by Linda Howe. All rights reserved. Printed in the United States of America. For information, address St. Martin's Publishing Group, 120 Broadway, New York, NY 10271.

This book is not intended as a substitute for the medical recommendations of physicians, mental health professionals, or other health-care providers. Rather, it is intended to offer information to help the reader cooperate with physicians, mental health professionals, and health-care providers in a mutual quest for optimal well-being. We advise readers to carefully review and understand the ideas presented and to seek the advice of a qualified professional before attempting to use them.

www.stmartins.com

The Library of Congress Cataloging-in-Publication Data is available upon request.

ISBN 978-1-64963-447-4 (trade paperback)
ISBN 978-1-64963-448-1 (ebook)

The publisher of this book does not authorize the use or reproduction of any part of this book in any manner for the purpose of training artificial intelligence technologies or systems. The publisher of this book expressly reserves this book from the Text and Data Mining exception in accordance with Article 4(3) of the European Union Digital Single Market Directive 2019/790.

Our books may be purchased in bulk for specialty retail/wholesale, literacy, corporate/premium, educational, and subscription box use. Please contact MacmillanSpecialMarkets@macmillan.com.

First published in the United States by Sounds True

First St. Martin's Essentials Trade Paperback Edition: 2026

10 9 8 7 6 5 4 3 2 1

This book is dedicated
to Jack and Dottie Howe, my perfect parents.
I love you.

CONTENTS

Welcome Anew 1

Introduction: Preparation 11
   How I Found the Akashic Records 11
   How to Use This Book 27
   Opening Meditation: The Pillar of Light 29

PART ONE: HOW TO READ THE AKASHIC RECORDS

1 An Introduction to the Akashic Records 35
   What Are the Akashic Records? 35
   Who Uses the Akashic Records, and Why? 42
   How Do People Access the Akashic Records? 43
   How Will We Access the Akashic Records in This Book? 46

2 Guidelines and Ground Rules for Reading the Akashic Records 49
   How Should I Prepare to Read the Akashic Records? 50
   What Kinds of Questions Work Best in the Akashic Records? 56
   What Should I Expect When I Open My Akashic Records for the First Time? 60
   What Kinds of Information Will I Get, and How Will I Get It? 61

3 **The Pathway Prayer Process   65**
   Understanding the Pathway Prayer Process: Reading for
      Yourself   67
   Reading Your Akashic Records for the First Time   79
   The Difference Between the Akashic Records and
      Intuition   80
   Exercise: The Akashic Records and Intuition   80
   Common Questions and Concerns about the Akashic
      Records   87
   Receiving the Help of Your Masters, Teachers, and Loved
      Ones   89
   Different Uses for the Akashic Records   91

4 **Reading the Akashic Records for Others   97**
   Understanding the Pathway Prayer Process: Reading for
      Others   99
   Tips on Reading for Others   104
   Developing an "Altitude of Consciousness"   109
   From Initiate to Beginning Practitioner   112

PART TWO: USING THE AKASHIC RECORDS TO HEAL YOURSELF AND OTHERS

5 **Energy Healing in the Akashic Records   115**
   How Does Energy Healing Occur in the Akashic
      Records?   117
   As an Akashic Records Practitioner, What Are My Roles and
      Responsibilities?   118
   The Three Levels of Healing in the Akashic Records   126
   How Can I Recognize the Three Levels of Healing?   131
   Exercise: The Three Levels of Healing (Working with Your
      Own Akashic Records)   131

Exercise: The Three Levels of Healing (Working in Someone Else's Akashic Records) 136

6 **Healing Ancestral Patterns in the Akashic Records** 143
Who Are My Ancestors? 144
How Do Souls Join Ancestral Lines? 145
What Is My Responsibility to My Ancestors? 147
How Can I Explore My Ancestors and Their Influence on My Life? 148
Exercise: Identify the Divine Intent of Your Lineage 149
Exercise: Explore the Space Between Lifetimes 150
Exercise: Identify and Clear Unwanted Ancestral Influences on the Present 152
Exercise: Healing a Difficult Bond or Tie 153

7 **Healing Past Lives in the Akashic Records** 155
What Are Past Lives? 156
How Does Past-Life Healing Occur in the Akashic Records? 159
Exercise: Working in the Akashic Records for Past-Life Healing 160
Exploring Positive Past Lives in the Akashic Records 166
Exercise: Exploring Positive Past-Life Experiences 167

8 **Life with the Akashic Records** 171
Akashic Assumptions 171
The Akashic Absolutes 177
Final Thoughts on the Akashic Records: The Past, the Present . . . and the Future 179

Gratitude 187

Further Resources   189

Appendix: The Pathway Prayer Process to Access
    the Heart of the Akashic Records   191

Glossary of Akashic Terms   195

Questions and Answers about the Akashic Records   201

Reflection Questions for Individuals or Groups   215

About the Author   223

Welcome Anew

When *How to Read the Akashic Records* was first published in 2009, I had taught the Akashic Records for more than a decade and felt a responsibility to share this powerful method with everyone seeking a more conscious connection with their Soul. With the treasured volume in my hands, I thought my work was done—having launched us into New Age consciousness with a technique for reliably connecting with the Akasha.

What I didn't know then, and could not possibly guess or imagine, was that this was merely the beginning of a new level of awareness and engagement with the world that would continuously unfold within me, through the particulars of my life, including parenting, partnering, daughtering, neighboring, and all the rest.

Sitting here in the turbulence of the 2020s, 2009 feels like an entirely different lifetime—and it was. Set free into a landscape of seekers exploring options for knowing the Truth, *How to Read the Akashic Records* launched a movement. My ignorance of all that was to come proved to be a blessing, freeing me to simply write and speak the Truth as it was being revealed to me. Life continued on. Luckily, the Akashic Records have been my constant companion and guide on the path toward learning to live an ordinary life as a regular person with a burning desire to lead an extraordinary, consciously Soul-led life unrestricted by dogma, institutions, or the past in any form.

When *How to Read the Akashic Records* was first published, I thought I was finished writing—time to put up my feet and bathe in the Light. But, instead, it sparked an entirely new adventure that invited me to pack my bags and travel the world! I was called to continue my exploration and experimentation, to keep going. It was wonderful, first going from city to city in the US, then eventually responding to invitations that led me to the ends of the Earth!

Having taught tens of thousands of students in person in countries including China, Japan, Brazil, and Russia, I look back on a memorable 2010 meeting with a smile. The world and I have changed quite a bit since then. That morning, the "A" Team (Jean Lachowicz and Susan Lucci) met to discuss the challenges we were facing in spreading the word about the Akasha, a term and concept very few were familiar with back then. What I had discovered was available to anyone with a sincere desire to know their own Soul was buried under old ideas. How could we let people know they were welcome to engage with our experiment, which so often revealed important and useful solutions? Our great challenge at the time was to make the Akasha understandable and accessible to curious folks yearning to have more conscious connections with their Souls—a necessary, but not so easy, task.

I can remember looking up "Akasha" on Amazon in 2009, but locating scant resources. Today, there are scores of Akashic references and now even books, many by old students of mine. It's funny to see that I have become a "keyword," and people are using my name to achieve rank and status in the field. Over the past decades, an avalanche of materials has hit the market. Some good, others not so good. This, of course, raises new questions and new challenges. What is the fundamental idea of the Records? What is the role of the Akasha in empowering people in their lives? On one hand, people come to the Records ready to dig in and discover. On the other hand, they come with a cluster of ideas that have nothing to do with the Records. These ideas have added to confusion and misperceptions that quickly become obstacles along the way.

The more experience I gained in the Akasha, the more I began to examine essential concepts, such as how to use the Records for personal and ancestral healing, how to live in the world while maintaining a strong spiritual point of view, and of course, how to spiritually manifest. With each new discovery, I created a class and wrote and recorded another book. My team grew, and we learned how to mine the treasures of the internet and technologies to train students and teachers all over the globe, even during a pandemic. While I am proud of each step of my path, I truly treasure *The Heart of the Akashic Records Revealed*, a collection of the entire curriculum presented to me in my Records over the past decades.

I certainly have learned and practiced many other spiritual technologies, and some practitioners mix the Records with other modalities, but I am uniquely devoted to the purity of the Akasha. I am a specialist and even designed and earned a doctorate in spiritual studies from the Emerson Theological Institute in 2015. What a wonderful and enjoyable surprise to be the first in the world to merit such a title!

Needless to say, as interest in the Records has grown, so have I. From young reader to teacher, I became a seasoned veteran, global citizen, world traveler, and wise sage, willing to seek, find, and spread the Light everywhere. Reflecting on my early days in the Records in 1994, I recall a vow I made to myself to do this work until it was no longer helpful or alive. Along the way, so many times I thought I was coming to the end of the road, but the Records tilted and revealed yet another magnificent vista. Like you, I am but a traveler on an infinite journey. This moment is one with this life. This life is one within this series of incarnations. My Soul is eternal.

UPDATES TO NEW EDITION

While the essence of accessing the Akashic Records using the Pathway Prayer Process© remains consistent, I have learned many new insights in the Records since 2009. Changes to the original manuscript reflect these updates. The back matter now includes a glossary to help explain key terms as well as a frequently asked questions section to address questions I hear students ask time and time again.

As we respond to the demands of these times with a refresh of *How to Read the Akashic Records* to meet the needs of today's readers, I want to briefly address a few major obstacles at the outset, confusions raised by students on every continent, from Europe to Asia and the Americas: (i) Karma, and how to find freedom from it, (ii) entities, other galaxies, and identities, going from one species to another, and (iii) obstacles that keep people from enjoying the quality of spiritual work they deserve, due mostly to their unreasonable expectations.

Understanding Karma

Understanding Karma—and finding freedom from it—is one of the most common difficulties people face as they sojourn through life, and it's a common difficulty people have when trying to understand the patterns they see in the Records. Karma itself is very simple: cause and effect. If I eat a chocolate cake every day for a month, then my jeans won't fit. The cause is me eating cake daily; the effect is gaining weight, which leads me to need larger jeans.

Some Karma has a rapid turnaround of cause and effect. However sometimes we see a karmic timeline play out over a longer time, from a few days to a few lifetimes. There are times when negative opinions we hold with regard to the people involved in any situation, including ourselves as well as our circumstances, will cause us to get stuck. This stuckness takes the form of pattern repetition until we make peace with the reality of the situation. Acceptance is the key to the resolution of all karmic patterns. As we make peace with who we are now, who we have been, and who we are becoming, the circle of life will continue.

It's a wonderfully predictive system—until we begin to judge or have negative opinions about the cause, effect, or people involved. Negativity is like Krazy Glue, stopping the cause-effect cycle. A pattern of action and reaction will repeat itself (sometimes over a series of lifetimes) until we make peace with ourselves, others, and all of the elements of the situation. Until the pattern is accepted, we will find a way to keep it at bay, whether with cake or any other behavior or substance. Becoming aware of and accepting the fact that "this is what I do, and it's not bad or good; it simply is" is the key to releasing the stuck pattern.

The idea of accepting karmic patterns to release them is often contrary to popular beliefs and cultural standards. No matter who or where, students globally seem to accept the notion of karmic retribution, punishment, or the need for public penance. This keeps them stuck in cycles expecting punishment. In truth, it's an essential matter of accepting the reality of a pattern—not assigning blame or refusing shame—and helping people truly change. This insight can be helpful when students encounter repeating patterns in their Records.

Entities, Other Galaxies, and Reincarnation

Many people want to consult their Akashic Records to see if they've been another kind of life form in a past life. The notion that humans have an ability to shift from one species to another over the course of their incarnations may or may not be accurate. Whether reincarnation across species is true or not, the Akashic Records do not have this information because the Record is the collective memory of Souls making their way through lives.

The same holds with the possibility that a human can live on other planets, may originate in a different starseed group, or any extra-terrestrial guidance. There is no information about these possibilities in the Akashic Records. The Record has no opinion on our personal beliefs, and it also does not hold that information.

I was surprised to learn that certain teachers were sharing that "blockages" to their students' progress were caused by entities. And that once they were free of these pesky entities, their progress as Akashic Records Practitioners would proceed. This is categorically false and, to my knowledge, a bit off the beam. Entities are bodies of fear that can gather around us when we are tired, burdened, or stressed. They often serve as obstructions for moving forward with a particular project or even with our Records work. We give our fears too much undeserved power in dissolving entities. Empowering our self-expression is a matter of ignoring the "entities" and becoming increasingly courageous on our individual paths. It broke my heart to learn that so many students had been stopped along the way by their fears, used against them by teachers who found a pat answer to any question or issue raised by their sincere students. The Akashic Records have no comment on many concerns that we humans bring to the conversation, like "Where am I from?" "What is my Soul's name?" "What's my Soul song?" etc.

Expectations When Accessing the Records

Traveling the world and meeting students of every background, race, and religion, I have learned a great deal about the issues that matter most, the problems humans encounter, and possible solutions to many of our presenting difficulties. What I've come to love about the Akasha is the emotional safety of the space. It is a dimension so accepting of us and the way we are that it becomes increasingly easier to be honest about our thoughts and feelings about everything presenting itself to us.

Working in the Records, I've learned the immense value of emotional safety for human beings and the Records' role in our growth and development. My observation is that when people experience acceptance, they relax and tell the Truth. In the Records, what moves the energy fastest is putting words to the Truth. As we describe what we are experiencing, the energy moves. When we are on the right track, it moves pretty quickly. When we are heading in the wrong direction, it seems to be stuck or dried up.

Many have come to understand that the Akashic Records are very complicated and secretive, and their ability to access and interpret them is due to them being special or some kind of exception. This is not true. Specialness is not an element of the Akasha. Every person has unique usefulness, a democratic, egalitarian approach; whereas specialness is both false and harmful to everyone involved. There is no hierarchy of status.

I've come to recognize over the course of our countless incarnations, every one of us will have experiences as leaders, followers, rich, poor, good, and even criminally bad. The question brought to my attention is "How do I love myself now?" The Akashic Records have revealed to me that everything I have ever done—and everything that has been done to me, around me, and even on the other side of the planet—is part of a magnificent vision empowering me to grow into unconditional love for myself, others, and life itself. The opportunity of all humans, without exception, is to love ourselves and others as we are loved and enjoyed by life.

When first working in the Records many moons ago, I did my best to cram my old beliefs into the Akashic framework. It was an epic failure. My favorite old idea was that over the course of time, I as a Soul would have "good" lifetimes and "bad," with the goal being to even out to a flat zero by the time I was finished. Imagine my shock learning that I was so wrong!

There is no cosmic scorekeeper, no faceless people in brown robes keeping the books, no library in the sky where I would locate a book with my name on a page for this incarnation. I was wrong about many glamorous ideas. Once reality took hold, I relished the freedom and hope inspired by the Akashic Records. This is a dimension of consciousness where everyone is valuable, whether they minister to sick people or sit on the couch, watch TV, and drink beer. I have come to live my life, not to judge others. What a huge relief and blessing to be free of those incorrect ideas!

My expectations were a serious impediment to my growth. I had ideas that the Records could be manipulated or rewritten, that it could erase people I no longer liked or change the past or the future. These expectations were crippling. None of them were true. The Records *slowly* revealed themselves to me one image at a time, many taking years of work to understand. Like any relationship, time is our friend. The longer I engage in the Records, the stronger they become. You will likely find the same. Slow down and enjoy the ride.

You may come to the Records with massive natural talent, or you may not. All that's needed is a sincere desire to know your Soul more than before and a willingness to learn. Set aside your expectations or ideas of how anything should be and settle in. It's a wonderful adventure, and it's yours to savor.

The time we are in is very difficult for many of us. Authoritarianism is on the rise, representative democracy is in decline, and the climate is downright frightening. The list of challenges is seemingly endless. As each of us is led to our own inner Light, Truth, and wisdom, we will uncover an arsenal of courage to step out in the world in the ways that only we can do. We'll bring to the moment the Truth as we recognize it, and we'll continue to grow into loving ourselves, others, and all of creation. This is why we are here. For now. For this.

We chose this time to be who we are and where we are. There are no accidents. The Universe has never made any mistakes, and it is not going to start now.

Here's another Truth I've discovered along the path: Life is best when enjoyed with others. I'm glad to be with you, knowing that together we can do what we cannot do alone.

INTRODUCTION

Preparation

HOW I FOUND THE AKASHIC RECORDS

My path to discovering the Akashic Records is mine. While I share these details, please know that your path will be unique and significant, so as you read this, consider your journey and all of its elements. Although there are certainly many commonalities bringing us together at this time, we also have our distinct differences, which are all precious and valuable. And so I begin . . .

To begin my conscious awakening, I did not have a near-death experience. It was more like I hovered near death spiritually for a period of years. The situation was grim, and I couldn't understand why it was happening. I had done everything right: I was a good girl who went to college, studied hard, and got good grades. I had a good job and a nice apartment. I had everything I thought I wanted . . . but I was miserable. Through sheer effort, I achieved what I set out to do, but my accomplishments couldn't quiet the scream echoing up from the canyon in my Soul. No matter how hard I tried, I never felt "good enough"; my efforts weren't cutting it. Sometimes I gave up and let myself be as "bad" as I could tolerate—to secure a feeling of "okay-ness," safety, or relaxation. But finally, in desperation, I prayed to a power I wasn't sure existed: "God, if you're there, help me. I can't take it anymore. Help. Please."

Within six weeks of that urgent prayer, a remarkable thing happened. I was lying on my bed, feeling sorry for myself and looking at a tree that had grown its way up to my third-floor window. Again, I called out for help: "How can my life look so good but feel so bad?"

Everything stopped. All the noise came to a halt, and a sense of calm relief took its place. When I looked at the tree, I knew we were connected; I could feel it. Twenty-three years old, raised in the city, and not one to spend much time in nature, I was stunned by the experience. For a few moments, I clearly felt myself to be one with the tree and every other thing I could see. The idea was immense yet comforting. I knew my life was not a fluke and that there was a God. Most importantly, I knew that this God liked me. God's *love* had never been an issue; I always knew that God loved me. But I had never been sure he *liked* me. In that miraculous moment, my fears were calmed and my questions answered. The feeling of being known fully and loved absolutely (and liked!) was unmistakable. The experience was so powerful and so profound, and the reality of it so overwhelming, that I'm still growing into it decades later.

Raised Catholic in the Midwest, my initial understanding of God was the "bearded old man in the sky." Feeling connected to the tree blew that idea apart. The God I encountered in that moment went far beyond my old concept. My new and expanded version of God was more of a force field than a person. This force field seemed to contain a host of distinct qualities that converged in that moment: positive, energizing power mixed with exquisite sensitivity; tender compassion; and kindness. There was a paradoxical sense of order without constriction, a meeting of exuberant joy, deep stillness, precise awareness, and reverence for the moment as well as an open, expansive inclusion of all that is, all that has ever been, and all that will ever be . . . occurring simultaneously.

Now, *this* was a God worth knowing! For a while, it seemed like there should be a better, more modern word to describe this power and its presence. Ultimately, though, I decided that the word "God" was the best term for me because it allowed space for this force field's unknowable, mysterious nature.

Since the episode with the tree, I have been blessed with many moments of heightened awareness. But that first conscious experience of the presence of God was the most riveting and transformational. In the blink of an eye, everything changed—*I* changed—and yet everything appeared the same. I knew that whatever that experience had been, I wanted more of it. I wanted to live my whole life from that place of being so known, so seen, so loved, and so liked. And so, my search began.

Mainstream Religion

I took off on my spiritual path with passion and enthusiasm. I sought to capture my initial experience and make it last—elongate it, duplicate it. My desire to re-experience that sense of Light, power, and presence took me to a number of places. First, I went to a full range of churches and temples, from Catholic Charismatic, where praying in tongues is the norm, to Buddhist temples, where people practice meditation and detachment. Within a short period of time, I recognized that all religions were and are fundamentally good, and to this day, I still participate in religious activities when I am moved to do so. But the revelatory experience I'd had was not there, nor was it being sought by others. Instead, I encountered lots of rules and lots of pressure to follow them. Men were in charge, and women served refreshments. That was not for me; the politics got in the way.

I was struggling to accept my sexual identity at the time and was fearful that the religious authorities would suspect the truth and banish me. It was clear then that traditional religion was not the path that would allow me to most deeply experience the presence of God as I had come to know it.

After my spiritual awakening, I felt so filled with grace that I easily let go of the habits, thoughts, and behaviors that had been standing in the way of my spiritual development. At the same time, I was given the energy I needed to develop new life patterns. My ridiculous partying fell away with relatively little effort on my part. I had tried to clean up my act before, but it had been beyond my capabilities. Being touched in this way, however, caused me to effortlessly move in a different direction. Anyone who has experienced this type of healing knows just how mysterious and miraculous it is. No human effort can compare.

For a period of time, perhaps as long as six months after the Light opened up inside me, I was wide open in consciousness. I felt as if I had entered a new dimension of living, and in fact, that was what had occurred. Everywhere I went, I would get a "hit," a sense of knowing that whatever I saw was God—an expression of the Oneness—and that I was one with it. Standing in line at the grocery store, I would quake at the realization that all who were present were one. Driving down beautiful Lake Shore Drive in Chicago, I easily accepted that everything I encountered was part of the whole and that I was a part of it. Passing housing projects jostled my world as that hit of awareness told me that this, too, was the face of God and that I was related to it.

My mother was a godsend during that time. She has a strong mystical awareness and is unafraid of spiritual reality. A progressive Catholic who has always been way ahead of her time, she supported me from her point of view, offering guidance and knowledge about the elements of her faith. Her support of me has never wavered, and for this, I am eternally grateful. Still, even her radical approach to a traditional path was not mine.

Exploring New Avenues

Having explored religion, I moved in the direction of self-help seminars. I attended tons and loved them all! Each brought me something I needed: understanding, people, or structure and organization. No matter where I went, I was blessed with something that supported my growth. Some of the workshops were positive, validating, and feel-good. Some were harsh, disturbing, and horribly uncomfortable. All of them contributed to my expanding awareness. What was missing from this pathway, however, was recognition of life's spiritual dimension.

So I continued my quest, accompanied by countless friends and comrades. I embraced therapy and bodywork of every variety. And I explored all kinds of readings. My generation made celebrities of spiritual readers, so of course I found myself at the table of many a soothsayer. And as with most avenues I explored, my experiences were usually wonderful.

When I was twenty-eight, I went with a friend to a Renaissance fair, where a tarot reader looked at my cards. That reading turned out to be a significant event for me, not because of the details of what the reader told me but because of how I *felt* when she finished. As I let the Truth of her words sink in, I experienced an amazing sense of personal liberation. If only I could offer that same feeling to others!

I left the fair with the notion of making my living by doing tarot readings. At the time, it seemed ridiculous. Tarot readers and others involved in spiritual divination all seemed so odd, so separate from mainstream life—almost misfits. It was frightening to think that if I did readings, I, too, would belong to that subculture. I had not yet reconciled within myself the notion of being a regular person in the world who happened to do tarot readings. No, at that time, it was an either-or situation: I could either travel in the real world or live on the outskirts.

A year or so later, another friend suggested I have a session with a woman in Texas who worked with the Akashic Records . . . whatever those were. This reader was quite popular, so I made a telephone appointment. I was told she would be able to tell me my Soul's purpose, and I certainly wanted to know what it was. At the time, my financial situation and my work life were so turbulent that I couldn't find a place to land. Every job I'd had during that period offered something I wanted, but on the whole, they were unsatisfying. I was truly baffled.

I called at the appointed time, and the woman launched into the reading. Her manner was warm, but between her thick accent and the new ideas she was presenting, I wasn't quite sure what she was saying to me. What I *did* know was that I had that feeling again, that distinct sense of being known and loved. The rest of the reading didn't really matter, and the thought crossed my mind that I would love to be able to do what she was doing.

Life kept moving forward. By the time I was thirty, I had resolved many of my difficult personal issues. Through the infinite love and strength available on an ongoing basis, I had been relieved of a terrible eating disorder and had met a wonderful life partner, with whom I continue to share my journey. When Lisa and I first met, she showed me how to read tarot cards. We spent countless hours throwing the cards. Her friend Steven had taught her how to decipher the tarot, and she simply passed it on. We had a blast, and for the next couple of years, I read the cards at every opportunity. While I was away at graduate school at the University of Illinois, I spent plenty of time developing my skills by doing readings for crazed graduate students.

I returned to Chicago and worked a regular job in title insurance by day, reading cards for people every chance I got. I hated my job. I tried to like it. I tried to make it work. I tried and

I tried and I tried . . . to no avail. I had to quit. I told myself that if I did, I would finish the Russian language requirement for my graduate degree in Russian history. Too terrified to admit the truth, I armed myself with a socially acceptable justification for quitting a perfectly fine job and gave my notice. But trying to learn Russian for the umpteenth time was downright painful, fully as intolerable as my title-insurance job. After lots of Soul-searching, and some wailing and gnashing of teeth, I took myself down off my homemade cross and quit Russian. Three seconds of blessed relief were mine before terror came to the fore. The moment of truth had arrived: I admitted to myself that I wanted to do readings—for a living. I wanted to be a professional tarot card reader.

To realize my dream, I cleaned houses by day and read tarot cards at coffee houses by night. It was such great fun! After a while, I set up an office in my home, and my practice began to grow. Then, an odd pattern began to take shape. I started to see then—as I see today—that the people who came to me for readings were generally bright and insightful. They would come in for their readings, and while we looked at their cards, we would "see" all kinds of things that would help them gain clarity and figure things out in their lives. We would congratulate ourselves as I walked them to the door, and then, about six to eight months later, they would return with the exact same issues.

Let me amend that: *Some* people returned with the same issues. There were actually two different groups of clients. One group only needed to gain some understanding to resolve their difficulties or move beyond their limitations. For them, the problem was a lack of knowledge, so knowledge *always* solved their problems. For the other group, though, the root of the problem was something else. For them, knowledge did not necessarily translate into power, and without the power they needed, the people in this group often remained stuck. So back to me they would come, and we would look at their cards again and repeat the same process. It was painful that these readings never seemed to "take," and I felt terrible.

My prayers grew desperate: "God, or whoever is in charge of my life, there must be a way for people to access the power they need to solve their problems. Clearly, knowledge is not enough. It's great as far as it goes, but it doesn't go far enough. Help! . . . And PS the solution can't lie with dogma or institutions because, as a group, the people who come to me don't like that."

By this time in my life, I had grown accustomed to spiritual responsiveness to my heartfelt prayers, and I knew that the answer would arrive at the perfect moment. I had no idea what the answer would turn out to be, yet I was open to any real solution.

Shamanic Journey

Not long after my prayer, a friend invited me to a shamanic drumming circle, but I didn't want to go. The thought of sitting barefoot in a circle with a bunch of folks in power-animal T-shirts seemed dreadful, not empowering. However, my friend raved about it, so I finally gave in. Picture it: There I was, reading tarot cards for a living, and I was afraid a shamanic drumming circle would be too weird. I had to laugh at myself!

A woman named Pat Butti held the meeting. She had the longest-running, most stable group in the area, so I felt pretty safe. She was great, the last thing I expected—frosted hair, a fluffy dog, and shag carpet on the floors. Welcoming energy was in the air. Pat briefly explained the journey we were about to embark upon. I thought it sounded hokey, and I figured nothing would happen for me, but I decided to be polite and participate to the best of my ability.

Within the first few beats of the drum, I was gone—off to another dimension that was as real to me as the clothes on my back. I felt it: the power to effect change—no dogma, no institution, just pure life force. *Okay,* I thought when I emerged from my trance, *now what?*

Within a few weeks, I was taking classes in classic core shamanism at The Foundation for Shamanic Studies, where I had the great fortune of training under Sandra Ingerman, the author of *Soul Retrieval*. My tarot practice yielded, and I began to offer shamanic healings. It was a marvelous way to bring power to people in need, to enable them to recover their lost life force for themselves. For the next five years, I worked as a shamanic practitioner in one-on-one sessions and in groups. It was wonderful.

You may already have guessed what's coming next—one path I'd found fulfilling was about to close and another was about to open.

One day, as I was leading a journey circle and calling to the directions as the leader does—essentially, calling for all persons present to get what they need—I heard myself calling out *to God* for protection and support. I was not calling to the spirits of the East, South, West, and North, as was the custom, but to God. Now, it's true that the directions and the animals—and all natural things—are expressions of the same Oneness, but somehow, without meaning to, I had left the shamanic structure. Then later, when I did a shamanic healing practice with someone, I heard myself telling God that this was his child, and we needed him to take care of the situation. Finally, standing in another drumming circle, I looked down at my hands and saw the physical signs of what had become an uncomfortable fit: I was one of the whitest white girls in the city! I'd best leave shamanism to others.

Akashic Records

It was time to pray my prayer of desperation again. This time, it went something like, "Okay, there has to be a way to access *both* knowledge and power that is simple and easy. No stuff to drag around—maybe just a prayer. Please help." And I did not doubt that help was on the way.

A few weeks later, I was on a panel presenting information about shamanism. Another woman was there to talk about the Akashic Records. I wasn't completely certain what she was talking about, as it was very esoteric, but there was something alluring about it, so I decided to take her two-day Beginning Akashic Records class. In it, she taught us how to open the Records by saying a specific prayer. When I followed her directions—*BAM!* I felt a very distinct shift. And there it was, that sense again, the sense of being known and loved. It was not as overwhelming as my original experience, but I recognized it and felt that, at long last, I was home.

What was especially compelling about this new experience was that it wasn't sensational. There were no spectacular phenomena: no talking in funny voices, no eyes rolling up into the head, none of that. There was just a simple, subtle, yet discernible shift within me that enabled me to access the dimension of consciousness I had been seeking. Over the years, this sense of love has proven to be reliably there for me. Anytime I wish to enter this wonderful state, all I have to do is say the prayer.

I began doing Akashic readings for my shamanic clients, and for the next two years, I worked with both systems. I did readings for myself almost daily and practiced Akashic readings on anyone who would let me. I felt like I was being "taken" by the Light and moved in a different direction. Whether reading for myself or someone else, I got the sense I had been striving to find. And there was more: Years of study came together for me. I had explored the writings of Joel S. Goldsmith and Alice Bailey, among others, and as a result, I was mentally prepared for the next stage of my journey. New Thought churches, Religious Science, and Unity—all doors I had opened previously—helped a great deal too. Everything I had experienced and learned supported me in my new realm. And everything continues to support me today!

In 1995, Lisa and I moved to the Olympic Peninsula with our young son, Michael, believing that this would be our home for the rest of our lives. We loved it; spectacular beauty surrounded us in the quaint Victorian seaport town of Port Townsend. There, on the edge of the map in a town of seven thousand people, my practice expanded. It was a place where people went to heal, so my work was embraced there. But adjusting to the move and raising a toddler were stressful for me. I felt blessed that my work was appreciated, but my client list quickly grew unmanageable. I found myself seeing so many people for consultations each week that this became stressful too. Finally, even though I loved it, doing so much of this work took its toll, and after a while, I began to feel like I was falling into a thousand pieces. Something had to give. I turned to prayer once more: "God, please help me. Show me what to do here."

Then, a revelation. I suddenly understood that many of the people who came to me for Akashic Records consultations could be doing the work for themselves; there was no obvious reason for them not to learn how to read the Records on their own. Teaching people how to do the work for themselves and others became a clear solution to my dilemma. If my clients could learn to access their own Records, they would be able to help themselves develop their own spiritual authority. They could shift from relying on me to following their own spiritual guidance, which would enable them to develop and mature. Then they could just come to me when they were stuck or in need of some outside support to move them along in their journey. My goal was, and always has been, to assist others in their quest, to help them find their own way rather than finding it *for* them (which, in truth, I cannot do anyway). I had never sought to foster an unnecessary dependence upon me, and I was relieved to have come upon this solution.

I believe that on a spiritual quest, there are distances we must travel on our own, and our challenge is to learn how to do that.

Then, there are other times when it's best to seek the counsel of others. Along the way, through trial and error, we learn when to go it alone and when to get assistance. And we learn that, ultimately, we are here to help one another.

So that was it: My prayer had been answered, and I had my solution. Teaching my clients to read their own Akashic Records was a way to empower them to be self-supporting. I'd then be free to focus on working with others who needed assistance from someone else. At the same time, I could delight in seeing my Akashic students grow into finding their own spiritual authority. It was perfect. And . . . it would have to wait.

Certified to Teach

Although my inner guidance was encouraging me to move toward teaching, the powers that be—both human and beyond human—thought it best to wait. I am not one to wait patiently! But I did because I needed a teacher to help me advance to the next level, to ground me in the practice solidly enough that I could pass it along effectively. For another full year, I continued doing consultations for others and juggling the rest of my life. And it was during that year that I met the teacher I needed.

I had a list of qualifications the right teacher would have to meet, and it was very specific and detailed. I wanted support, guidance, and instruction from someone I admired, respected, and enjoyed. I also wanted someone with whom I felt free to be honest and around whom I felt safe enough to be vulnerable, yet who recognized my strong points as well. Ideally, this person would have everything I wanted and would be able to instruct me. One day, Mary Parker arrived, and she turned out to be that kind of teacher for me.

As soon as I met Mary, the way forward opened up, and things quickly fell into place. Mary had received a "sacred prayer." One of the ways in which people have engaged the Akashic Records is through the use of sacred prayers. These prayers have been given to individuals as their "access codes," which enable them to enter, experience, and exit the Records successfully. This sacred prayer tradition is based on the vibrational patterns of specific words and phrases, which together establish a vibrational light-grid—an energetic bridge—to a particular region of the Akashic Records. Each prayer emits a Soul-level signal that contacts and beckons individuals who resonate with the prayer's vibration. Since those individuals are energetically related to the particular tones, lights, and sounds of that prayer, they can use it, if they so desire, to interface with the Records. Currently, there are many people in active relationships with the Akashic Records, and they use a variety of sacred prayers with wonderful results.

When Mary and I met on the phone, we immediately recognized one another, and I made arrangements for her to come to Port Townsend to teach a beginners' class. At least I assumed *she* would be doing the teaching—but no. The weekend arrived, more than thirty-five people assembled in the community center . . . and she put me in front of the class.

With Mary Parker's blessing, I became certified to teach the Akashic Records using her sacred prayer. People came, classes happened, and through my own Records, advanced work was revealed to me. This time in my life could not have been more exciting, demanding, or fabulous. Here was a way to pass something on to others that would allow them to access their own spiritual authority—a simple, nondramatic, reliable method to support those who are called to this Light as a path of consciousness development.

It has been particularly meaningful for me to teach people how to become both spiritually independent and Divine-reliant at the same time. I know there are times when we must seek the counsel of others. On the spiritual path, we work with the duality of doing for ourselves and letting others help us. Knowing *what* to do *when* is a skill of spiritual maturity. Being riddled with self-doubt, on the other hand, is a most uncomfortable way to live. I've been there. During that time when I was confused and unsettled—when I was on my way toward a more authentic spiritual commitment, but at times doing things to avoid it—I was going outside of myself to as many readers and witch doctors as I could find. I was seeking, striving, *longing* for someone to tell me what my purpose was, what God wanted me to do, what the Universe expected from me. It was awful. Essentially, I wanted someone else, divinely inspired or not, to tell me *who* to be and *how* to be in this life. The idea of discovering those things myself scared the daylights out of me. *What if I steered myself wrong?* It was a responsibility issue, really. If I followed other people's advice and things didn't work . . . well, it would be *their* fault, not mine.

Pathway Prayer

As time passed in Port Townsend, it became clear that our family was better suited to a more urban environment. Still, it was with great sadness that we packed up and headed back to the Midwest. When I returned to the Chicago area, my work expanded. I saw individuals and held classes. Reading my own Akashic Records had given me access to priceless resources: classes, ideas, and suggestions about their implementation.

One of my driving questions had always been how to be both spiritually aware and a responsible participant in everyday life, and that question still called for an answer. I'd seen so many people who were either one or the other. I knew intuitively that the spiritual force I had found was not meant to take me away from life, but rather to enhance my ordinary living. Spending time in my Records, I sought guidance on this topic as well as many others.

After I'd been teaching in the Midwest for a few years, I got an unexpected call from Mary Parker. She let me know that she was restructuring her relationships with the people who used her sacred prayer to teach the Akashic Records. By now, I'd had a great deal of experience with the Records, and the many changes she had decided to implement didn't make sense to me. I realized that I could not incorporate her ideas into my work because the guidance I was receiving was different from hers, so out of respect for Mary and her lineage, and out of respect for myself, I knew I had to step away. I stopped teaching the Akashic Records, continuing only my work with individuals. It was a difficult transition because a part of me wanted to belong to the community I had come to know. However, the cost of belonging would be dishonoring my own spiritual Truth, and disregarding my own guidance was out of the question.

For the next eighteen months, I prayed, cried, wondered, and navigated a great internal maelstrom. At the center of the storm, I struggled with my relationship to the God of my understanding. Out of that struggle came the foundation for what I called "the God classes." Though initially what I had created offered a systematic way I could resolve some of my outgrown ideas about God, I saw that this approach could benefit others—and with good reason. In my teaching of the Akashic Records, I had observed that those who were comfortable with their God did deep, rich work in the Records. Those who were uncomfortable with their God, however, had a harder time working in the Records. So the God classes helped us all.

During the summer of 2001, as I prayed furiously for help, I received the recurring message that I must teach the Akashic Records! This was fascinating. I kept telling God, in no uncertain terms, that this was out of the question, but the persistent notion would not leave me. The first weekend in September, in the midst of a spiritual temper tantrum, a prayer came to me. It broke through my ranting, and my mind went still as the words and rhythm quietly dominated the space. Saying that prayer opened me up to a powerful realm in the Records, where my heart softened and my mind lined up to support my heart. I had moved to a new level with the Pathway Prayer. It was awesome.

After I received my own sacred prayer from the Records, I made an appointment with my assistant, Christina, to talk by phone on the morning of September 11, 2001. I planned to share the prayer with her and get her reaction to it. That morning, while we talked, the Twin Towers of the World Trade Center in New York City were being hit, and a new dimension of consciousness was being opened up for millions. I will have more to say about this astonishing convergence later, but I like to think of the Pathway Prayer I received, which allowed me to access the Heart of the Akashic Records, as an expression of the higher vibrations that were released that day.

I had so much to learn! The Pathway Prayer intensely engages the heart, and this requires practitioners to be very active in their own inner work. The clearer and more open their hearts, the stronger their connection to the Light. When hearts are open, this prayer offers an accessible portal to the Akashic Records. I was eager to follow the guidance I was getting from the Records, so I soon set up the Center for Akashic Studies and taught classes there—lots of classes. To this day, new ideas and understandings keep coming through to me from the Records, and I act upon them to the best of my ability. As new technologies are developed, I learn how to reach more students in more ways. Invitations keep coming from around the world, so I have taught my method to thousands of students from a variety of backgrounds, beliefs, and hometowns. As I have learned more, I have developed more classes and published more books. My team evergreened my work for future generations. The wisdom streaming from the Akasha is unlimited!

What has been most striking to me about this particular pathway into the Records is that compassion and acceptance are dominant. With every reading I do—for myself or someone else—I get a fresh dose of Light and love. It may sound corny, but it's true. These energies have helped me grow beyond self-rejection and self-abandonment and into greater self-love. And with a greater awareness of the love present within me, it is only natural for me to want to share more love with others.

Over the years, I have had many readings with practitioners from a variety of disciplines. Astrologers, aura readers, intuitives, and channelers all offered many positive and helpful ideas. However, I often encountered the same problem with these readings. No matter who the reader was or what method of divination they used, I was told emphatically that if I would only "love myself," everything would be just fine. Being urged to do this didn't make it any easier to get to that place within myself. Though I knew they were correct and sincere in their desire to assist me, I didn't know how to translate their words into an experience of accepting and respecting myself for who I was at the time.

Now, through the grace of an infinitely generous and loving God, I have grown to love myself more today than ever before. Through this pathway, into the Heart of the Akashic Records, I have enjoyed the distinct sense of my own goodness and the goodness of others, as well as the experience of being seen, known, and loved—and most important—liked. It is my sincere wish that this book will lead you to the source of Light from which these wonderful qualities emanate: the Akashic Records.

HOW TO USE THIS BOOK

I'm thrilled that you found your way to this book about learning to read the Akashic Records. I can tell you with certainty that if your experiences in the Records are anything like mine and my students', this work will blow you away—literally. It will blow away the misperceptions you've held about the world up to this point in your life. It will blow away the fears and excuses that have kept you from moving forward. And it will blow you *into* a new place of understanding, insight, love, and peace—a place that allows you to embrace your life and everything about it.

So, congratulations! At some point, you made a deliberate decision to deepen your spiritual connection and expand your experience on this planet. Now is the perfect time to begin, and this book is your perfect tool. It contains the curriculum for my Beginning Class and walks you through the entire process of learning to read the Akashic Records. The book is divided into two parts: Part 1 is preparation, and includes very important grounding and preliminary information about how to read the Akashic Records. Part 2 offers techniques and exercises for using the Records to heal yourself and others.

As you work your way through this book, you'll probably read some parts only once. Other parts, however, will become stopping places you'll revisit many times. However you choose to use this book, the information it presents is cumulative—it builds upon itself—so please read it all the way through at least once.

In the back of the book is a treasury of resources designed to empower you on your way. A glossary of terms used while working in the Akashic Records is followed by the most commonly asked questions in beginning and advanced classes, along with answers. As your foundation, this volume holds everything you need to launch your quest in the Records. For additional training and resources, please take a look at my other books and my website, LindaHowe.com.

It is my heartfelt hope that you will make extensive use of this book, that you will give the spiritual opportunity before you a fair try. With the book as your guide, you can follow the Light in ways you never dreamed of before.

And now, our journey begins. . . .

AN OPENING MEDITATION

I'd like to take this opportunity to welcome you to an exciting new dimension of spiritual knowledge. This dimension is so subtle—with such a light and quick vibration—that it will cause an energetic shift in your consciousness. As this shift occurs, it will allow you to move out of your ordinary ways of perceiving so you can access the extraordinary and interface with the Divine!

To facilitate this shift in consciousness, I start each of my Beginning Classes with a meditation. This meditation helps us ground ourselves in an energetic pillar of Light that lovingly holds us steady as we move into our work. So please find yourself a comfortable chair in a quiet room. Seat yourself squarely, with your back straight and your feet on the floor. Then read through the following meditation at a pace that feels comfortable to you. Many people use this Pillar of Light Meditation before going into their Records or reading the Records of others. It is not required, but it can be helpful. The choice is always yours.

OPENING MEDITATION

The Pillar of Light

As you sit with your feet flat on the floor, let your chair hold you up and support you. Get a sense of where you are and where your body is. Now, rub your hands together and begin to draw energy up from the heart of the earth. Draw it up from the very center of the planet, through the soles of your feet, and allow it to travel up through your body, up through your legs, up through your trunk, into your neck, and up into the cavity of your skull. Allow the energy to press into the lining of your skull.

While still rubbing your hands together, you might notice that the energy has been traveling down your arms and into your hands. By now, your hands should be warm. Use them to clear your aura—the energy field around your body. Physically brush off your body, clearing away any vibration on you or around you that isn't yours. Send it into the earth, where it can be absorbed and transmuted. Then, when you're finished, put your hands palms-up in your lap or on the armrests of the chair.

Now, allow yourself to become aware of the infinitely powerful and loving source of Light that is always there, hovering about eighteen inches above your head. As you become more aware of the Light, it becomes more activated, and it rains down over you—in front, behind, and on both sides. The Light clears away anything on you or around you that interferes with your ability to experience your own goodness.

As the Light moves from head to toe, it gathers under your feet and begins to swell. It begins to establish for you a platform of Light that holds you up in this place, at this time. It doesn't bind your feet, but it does hold them and support them.

Then, the Light begins to fill your energy field. This is an egg-shaped space that extends all the way around you, about eighteen inches in every direction—in front, behind, and on both sides. The Light begins to fill that space . . . up to your ankles . . . your knees . . . your hips . . . all the way up to your shoulders and over the top of your head, so now you are sitting inside a pillar of Light.

Take a moment now to let the Light do its work on you. First, by its natural magnetic property, the Light draws from you anything within that doesn't support you: any physical pain, stress, or distress; any emotional turbulence, worry, or chaos; and from your mind, any thoughts that might be scaring you or upsetting you. The Light can draw all of that from you. It can draw from you anything within that is interfering with your experience of the ever-present inner peace. You don't have to tell the Light what to do. The Light is an infinite intelligence that knows exactly what you need at this moment. Just let it do its work. . . .

And while the Light is drawing from you through its magnetic nature, at the same time, by its radiant nature, it is radiating itself into you. And as the Light radiates into you from every angle possible—in front, from above, from below—and as it passes through the boundary of your skin, the Light becomes exactly what you need. So if what you need is courage, the Light will become that. Perhaps you need comfort. The Light will become that. Open yourself up to observe the Light as it becomes what you need in the moment. Take a few moments to allow this to happen. . . .

By now, you should be in a state of reasonable balance and be ready to move forward. Bring your attention back to this moment, then continue reading.

PART ONE

HOW TO READ THE AKASHIC RECORDS

An Introduction to the Akashic Records

WHAT ARE THE AKASHIC RECORDS?

Traditionally, the Akashic Records were understood as a dimension of consciousness that contains a vibrational record of every Soul and its journey. This vibrational body of consciousness exists everywhere in its entirety and is completely available at all times and in all places. As such, the Records are an experiential body of knowledge that contains everything every Soul has ever thought, said, and done over the course of its existence, as well as all its future possibilities.

Let's break the above definition into smaller parts, starting with the meaning of "dimension of consciousness." A dimension of consciousness is a realm of the unseen world that we humans can identify and experience through its qualities, characteristics, or traits. For example, the dream state is a dimension of consciousness that contains different levels of sleep activity that humans can identify and experience. Other dimensions of consciousness can be identified as different "regions" of the mind—the conscious and subconscious, the zone of memory, areas of musical or mathematical abilities—and areas of the brain that govern our physical capabilities. Still other dimensions of consciousness are the different states of relaxation that are measured by brain activity. What all these dimensions of consciousness have in common is that, although they are unseen, we know they exist.

In the process of accessing, or "opening," the Akashic Records, we transition from a state of ordinary human consciousness to a state of universal consciousness, in which we recognize our Oneness with the Divine at all levels. This state of consciousness allows us to perceive the impressions and vibrations of the Records. In this way, the Records have served humanity throughout its unfolding by being an extra-ordinary state through which we can receive spiritual illumination at a manageable rate and integrate it into our human experience. Because of this integration, we can quite literally say that accessing the Akasha allows us to glimpse heaven on earth!

As time has passed, I've come to use a different definition. The Akashic Record is a vibrational archive of every Soul and its journey as human. The Record is invisible to the naked eye. We do not see it, and there is no library, but we can feel it. Just as an archive is a collection, the Record is a collection of every Soul in existence. This is good news for most of us; it means that no other person has the authority to delete us from the Record. And by the same token, we never gain access to eliminate any other person from this resource. Finally, the Record is the collective memory of our Souls' journeys as humans on Earth. It does not comment on whether or not we exist in other dimensions or as extra-planetary beings or if we shift from one species to another. These concepts may or may not be true, but they are definitely not a part of the Record. The Akashic Record is composed exclusively of the Soul's journey as human.

Now, on to the meaning of "Akasha." The introduction to *The Aquarian Gospel of Jesus the Christ* by Levi H. Dowling has perhaps the best description of the word:

> *Akasha* is a Sanskrit word, and means *[p]rimary sub-stance*, that out of which all things are formed . . . It is the first stage of the crystallization of spirit . . . This Akashic, or primary substance, is of exquisite fineness and is so sensitive that the slightest vibrations of an ether any place in the Universe register an indelible impression upon it.

When we talk about the Akasha, the primary substance, we are referring to energy in its first and earliest state—*before* it has been directed by our individual thoughts and affected by our emotions in this lifetime. This energy is a quality of Light in both the physical and spiritual senses. It is a quality of aliveness, or vitality, individualized uniquely as specific Souls.

Although Akasha is a Sanskrit word, the Akashic Records are noted in many sacred texts. Following are several references:

> "You keep count of my wanderings; put my tears into Your flask, into Your record."
> —The Jewish Bible Tanakh, Psalm 56:8–9

> ". . . then I said, 'Behold, I come; in the volume of the book it is written of me; I delight to do Your will, O my God; yes. Your law is within my heart.'"
> —The Amplified Bible, Psalm 40:7–8

"... then I said, 'Behold, Here I am, coming to do Your will, O God ... [to fulfill] what is written of me in the volume of The Book.'"
—The Amplified Bible, Hebrews 10:7

"You had scrutinized my every action, all were recorded in your book, my days listed and determined, even before the first of them occurred."
—New Jerusalem Bible, Psalm 139:16

"... the book in which men's actions, good and bad, are recorded, The Book of Life."
—New Jerusalem Bible, Revelation 20:12

"May we and the entire House of Israel be remembered and recorded in the Book of Life, blessing, sustenance, and peace."
—*Mahzor for Rosh Hashanah and Yom Kippur: A Prayer Book for the Days of Awe*, Rabbi Jules Harlow, editor

"And Jesus opened up to [the disciples] the meaning of the hidden way, and the Holy Breath, and of the light that cannot fail. He told them all about the Book of Life, the Rolls of Graphael, the Book of God's Remembrance, where all thoughts and words of men are written down."
— *The Aquarian Gospel of Jesus the Christ*, 158:3–4

The Akashic Records are the Light Body of universal self-awareness. As such, they contain the universal consciousness, with its three main components of mind, heart, and will. The Records also contain the radiant vibrations of Light that all things generate. Every time we access the Records, our awareness is affected by this quality of Light, and we become "en-Lightened" by it. When this happens, the effects of the Light become evident in our thoughts and emotions (and in those of our clients), and we begin to experience an increased sense of peace and well-being.

The Akashic Records are governed and protected by a group of nonphysical Light Beings called the Lords of the Records. These beings ensure the safety and integrity of the Records. They determine not only who can access the Records, but what information they can receive. The Lords of the Records work with the Masters, Teachers, and Loved Ones—who serve as the interface between the Akashic and earthly realms—by "downloading" to them the information that they will relay during each Akashic Record reading.

Though the Lords of the Records and the Akashic Masters are nonphysical beings, some of the Teachers and all of the Loved Ones have existed as humans on earth. When you work in the Akashic Records, you will never see the Lords of the Records, nor will you see the Teachers and Loved Ones as they existed in human form, but you may sense their energetic presence if a Teacher or Loved One deems it appropriate and necessary to come forward and relay certain information. Usually, however, the Masters, Teachers, and Loved Ones prefer to remain anonymous so we learn to rely on the *energy* of the Records rather than on specific identities in the Records.

In chapter 3, I will discuss in more detail the roles of the Lords of the Records and the Masters, Teachers, and Loved Ones. However, as you may have surmised from the preceding description, working in the Akashic Records requires an understanding and acceptance of the concept of reincarnation. From the perspective of the Records, all Souls are eternal. At this level of understanding, the Records hold the archive of each Soul as it has existed from lifetime to lifetime as different human beings on the earth plane while evolving throughout time and space. A human incarnation occurs as a specific manifestation of the perfect blueprint of the Soul. The idea of the human experience is to become, in the physical, the perfect self that already exists in the Akasha at the Soul level. Growing into the awareness of one's spiritual nature and being able to anchor that awareness in the physical and become that optimal self on the earth plane takes time—many lifetimes, in fact. In the Records, we are able to see and register our various incarnations. So in essence, the Akashic Records are both the perfect Soul-level blueprint and the catalogue of experiences of an individual Soul as it grows into awareness of itself as a spiritual being—divine in nature and manifesting in the physical earth-arena.

It is easy to understand why the Akasha is often called "the Records." The Akasha is organized in a way that allows us humans to interact with this spiritual resource and gain insight, guidance, and understanding within earthly time and space. In order for the Records to be accessible to us, they are organized by current legal names. This way, whatever lifetime we are in, we can gain entry and find the blueprint, or the "Record," of our individual Soul and examine the path to its realization.

While it is true that the Akashic Records of every Soul exist everywhere all at once and are entirely accessible, it would not be useful to have total access to a Soul's Records during a single Akashic Record reading. The information would be so vast and overwhelming that deciphering it would be nearly impossible and could do more harm than good.

Every name has a distinct vibrational quality, so when we open a particular Soul's Records, we use the name that the Soul is currently using in this lifetime. The vibration of that name then makes available to us the "set of Records" that contains the information that will be most relevant during the reading. It's no wonder the Akashic Records have been likened to a "cosmic internet" that allows us to "Google" specific information when we open a person's Records.

The energy of the Records moves on the formed, or spoken, word. As an Akashic Records reader describes what they are receiving from the Records, the process flows. The spoken words facilitate the movement of the energy, the relationship to the story at hand, and the client's thoughts, feelings, and subsequent actions. When you work in your own Records and assign words to what is occurring—whether through thought, writing, or speech—you are facilitating the same flow of energy and information.

The Akashic Records are always changing and expanding. As our Souls evolve over time, our Records adjust to reflect our growth and are in a continual state of refinement as we align with our perfection and manifest that perfection in our earthly lives. Therefore, we can look at the Records as an intermediary body of all past, present, and future possibility, probability, and eventuality. Through them, we can derive understanding and direction as we open up within ourselves on our journey to become our optimal selves in the physical world.

The Akashic Records are nonintrusive and noninvasive. They are not aligned with a particular personality or entity, nor are they governed or owned by any human organization or institution. Therefore, they are not the exclusive domain of any religion or metaphysical wisdom school; rather, they are available to all.

Because the Akasha is the primary substance out of which all thoughts are formed, the Records are interpreted in different ways by different cultures, religions, and organized belief systems. What is commonly agreed upon by all is the Akashic energy itself, which is manifested and generally recognized as love, light, peace, power, beauty, harmony, joy, strength, order, and balance.

WHO USES THE AKASHIC RECORDS, AND WHY?

For centuries, the Akashic Records were the exclusive domain of mystics, saints, and scholars—and rightly so. Infinite power and wisdom are available in the Records, and they have been entrusted to those who are well prepared for the responsibility of deep knowing. In both Eastern and Western traditions, mystery schools have prepared seekers for esoteric knowledge. Trainings were known to be rigorous and exacting in order to ensure the sanctity of the work, protecting both the initiate and the dimension of consciousness.

Times have changed, however. The collective consciousness of the human race has grown, evolved, and matured. In the process, humanity has moved from the age of dependence on a spiritual "parent" to spiritual independence and responsibility. This spiritual independence is marked by individuals knowing that they have direct access to their spiritual source and can use their independence to cultivate that relationship. As we continue to forge new paths both *in* and *to* the Akashic Records, more people than ever before are being drawn to their Light. Today, anyone with a conscious commitment to seeking and spreading Divine Light and healing can access this body of wisdom, insight, and guidance.

In the mid-twentieth century, clairvoyant Edgar Cayce (1877–1945) was the only person who read the Akashic Records publicly. He was known as the "sleeping prophet" because his method of accessing the Records was to put himself into a sleep state that allowed him to shift his consciousness and access the Akasha. While in this state, Cayce relayed information while someone else took notes. Upon awakening, he shifted back to his ordinary state of consciousness and remembered nothing of what had transpired.

For forty-three years, Cayce gave daily Akashic Records readings. Today, those readings—more than fourteen thousand of them—are available to the public and provide a wealth of information about the Akashic Records themselves, as well as answers to thousands of questions related to health and spirituality. What is significant for us today about Cayce's work is that he popularized the Akashic Records. Though theosophist H. P. Blavatsky (1831–1891) and anthroposophist Rudolf Steiner (1861–1925) referred to the Akashic Records in their writings, it was not until Cayce's work in the early to mid-twentieth century that Akashic Records readings became a familiar practice in the movement of consciousness development.

Today, tens of thousands of people have powerful relationships with the Akashic Records. While some people work in their Records strictly for personal growth and development, others use their Records to support artistic endeavors, such as photography, pottery, painting, writing, and composing. Businesspeople use the Records to help manage their companies or careers, and parents use the Records for guidance and support in parenting.

HOW DO PEOPLE ACCESS THE AKASHIC RECORDS?

The variety of methods that people use today to access the Akashic Records corresponds to the variety of spiritual resources. The Pathway Prayer Process that I present in this book is part of the "sacred prayer" tradition of accessing the Records. In this tradition, individuals find their way into the Records through the Light and sound vibrations of spoken words. The different prayers that people have developed are "access ramps" that lead to different areas of the Records.

While some people use prayers to access the Records, others gain access through hypnosis. Still others have been able to tap into the Records by using the symbols of the healing practice known as Reiki. And yes, there are those who have been able to access the Records as a result of their meditation practices and other forms of consciousness development. All ways into a conscious relationship with the Akashic Records are good and valid. What matters most about the method you choose is that it aligns with who you are as a person and allows you to comfortably experience the most effective readings possible. In picking up this book, you were led to the Pathway Prayer Process to Access the Heart of the Akashic Records© because this particular method can work for you. You would not have been guided to this method if it were not an effective resource for you, so relax; you're on the right path. When you're ready to take your first steps toward opening your Akashic Records, you will be guided and supported. After all, the Universe is on your side and is conspiring for your success!

Through my work as both a teacher and a reader for the Records, I have learned that most of the people attracted to the Pathway Prayer Process have had experiences with the energy of the Akashic Records at some earlier time. However, these may have been "accidental" and could not be duplicated easily, so the Records have not been a reliable spiritual resource for them. Consciously and deliberately using the Pathway Prayer Process, however—which is, in effect, a spiritual code—will allow you authority over the process so you can access the Records whenever you choose. In essence, using the Pathway Prayer Process gives you a way to access the Records for yourself and others consciously, responsibly, directly, and at will—and this is unprecedented in human history.

While the Akashic Records have always been available, they have not always been available to everyone. Instead, the Records have long been the domain of a very select group who would interact with the Akasha on their own behalf or on behalf of their communities. When we talk about the New Age in regard to the Akashic Records, we are talking about the fact that this is the time when secular people choose their own resources, including the Records, and walk their own spiritual paths. The days of spiritual immaturity, "spoon-feeding," spiritual oppression, and victimization are over. We are in a new time of learning how to be in conscious relationship with our own spiritual authority. A hundred years ago, this was not a possibility. Actually, it would have been considered scandalous.

It is curious that at the first writing of this book, there were not many books about the Akashic Records in circulation. Remarkably, this book was the very first of its kind that actually taught an explicit method for reading the Akashic Records.

In the second half of the twentieth century, a few books emerged that identified and described the Akashic Records. Their emergence coincided with the first stage of educating the mass consciousness about the existence of the Records and their potential as a spiritual resource. From that first stage of books, there are two I recommend. The first is by Robert Chaney, the founder of Astara, a metaphysical wisdom school in California. His book, *Akashic Records: Past Lives & New Directions,* likens the Akashic Records to a computer system and uses computer terms to discuss different elements of the Records. The second book is by Kevin Todeschi of the Association for Research and Enlightenment (A.R.E.), an organization that studies and promotes the work of Edgar Cayce. Todeschi's book, *Edgar Cayce on the Akashic Records: The Book of Life*, provides an illuminating perspective on how Cayce worked in the Records, the kinds of information he received during readings, and how that information was utilized.

Among books published more recently, I recommend an exciting work called *Science and the Akashic Field: An Integral Theory of Everything* by philosopher Ervin László. This book takes a scientific approach to identifying and validating the existence of the Akashic Records, or "A-Field." For more, please consult the Further Resources section in the back matter.

The reason I wrote this book on how to read the Akashic Records is to give you a tool you can hold in your hands, something you can use to move yourself forward on your spiritual path. This is the time. It is our time in history, and we are the people—the vanguard of the New Age, individuals who take responsibility for their own spiritual awareness and their conscious relationship with the God of their understanding. This is not channeling in the old-fashioned way. As Akashic readers, we "channel" by allowing the energy of the Records to move through our bodies, hearts, and minds. We channel energy and information directly from the Akasha, not from entities or personalities from other dimensions.

As I mentioned earlier, most of the people who come to me for Akashic readings or classes show up because, at some deep level, they are familiar with the Records already. They are responding to an inner prompting that this is their time to be active and conscious in their spiritual development. The Records always meet people where they are. You will only be attracted to this book if it is your time to learn to read the Records. You may find when you begin reading the Records that they feel familiar to you. Make yourself right at home.

HOW WILL WE ACCESS THE AKASHIC RECORDS IN THIS BOOK?

In this book, we will use the Pathway Prayer Process to Access the Heart of the Akashic Records. As I mentioned in the preface, I was given the Pathway Prayer by my Akashic Masters, Teachers, and Loved Ones in September 2001, and I shared it for the first time with my assistant Christina just as the Twin Towers collapsed on September 11. There was an opening in the collective heart of humanity at that time because that was the single-most aggressive attack on American soil in history, and our former sense of invincibility was shattered—replaced with a new sense of vulnerability.

In 2001, the movement for inner spiritual awakening grew rapidly in the United States. The increasing awareness of humanity's interconnectedness in the American psyche corresponded to the wounding of the United States and the subsequent opening of the heart of all humanity. This particular prayer is a focal point for human attention. It anchors and stabilizes that opening in the heart space and allows us to access it more deeply. Since so many people's hearts were opened that day as they reached out to each other across the world, I believe that this prayer, too, opened a pathway into the core, the Heart, of the Records, which is the seat of unconditional love within the Akashic body of wisdom.

Why use a prayer to access the Akashic Records? Since they exist within the realm of spirit, they are considered a "spiritual" entity, so this particular domain of consciousness is best accessed and achieved through the spiritual action of prayer. As a spiritual approach, prayer involves our entire being: the mental process of directing and focusing our thoughts, the physical act of speaking them, and the emotional response that we feel in regard to our message or request. These things combine to create a spiritual experience, through which we reach across time and space and make conscious contact with Divine Spirit. So even if we don't feel spiritual while praying, the act itself is an acknowledgment of spiritual Truth and the desire to live and act from that place at that time.

Teaching the Pathway Prayer Process to thousands of students over the past several decades, I have watched them use it to usher in a new and higher dimension of consciousness, not only for themselves, but for those whose Records they read. It has been an exciting and miraculous process, the effects of which are being felt across the planet. And now I am excited to offer the Pathway Prayer Process to you.

2

Guidelines and Ground Rules for Reading the Akashic Records

In this chapter, I set out some guidelines to facilitate your work in the Records. These are meant to help you prepare for the most enlightening experiences possible. They encourage kindness and respect in communication, responsible use of time, and appropriate ways of combining the Records with other spiritual systems. The guidelines also provide suggestions for formulating your questions before a reading, and they describe the kinds of information you might receive, as well as how you might receive them.

I've compiled these guidelines from a few different sources, including Mary Parker; my own Akashic Masters, Teachers, and Loved Ones; and my experiences while teaching others to read the Records. Through the years, I have found that there are ways of working in the Records that support more accurate, effective readings, and I pass this information to you so you can be successful in your practice.

HOW SHOULD I PREPARE TO READ THE AKASHIC RECORDS?

The way you choose to live your life has no bearing on your ability to access the Akashic Records. However, deciding the best way to approach an Akashic Records reading is a conscious and deliberate matter that requires conscious and deliberate choices. The following guidelines will help you make choices that allow you to work responsibly in the Records. They will facilitate your shift into the Akashic field of consciousness and support you in receiving information as clearly and strongly as possible. Although I strictly follow these guidelines as a way to prepare for readings, I am in no way asking you to alter your personal lifestyle and follow the guidelines daily. If you like to drink alcohol, for example, that is totally your choice. I'm merely instructing you to abstain from alcohol twenty-four hours before giving a reading. The first guideline below will explain why this is important.

Guidelines for Reading the Akashic Records

1. **Do not consume recreational drugs or alcohol for twenty-four hours before opening the Records.**
   The general understanding about drugs is this: If you are taking a prescription drug that your body needs for balance and healing, that drug will not interfere with your ability to read the Records. However, recreational drugs or alcohol will work against you in a reading because they'll compromise your energy field and make its edges "wobbly" or "shaky," which will distort your perception. (Think about what happens when you view yourself in a fun house mirror: You don't see an accurate image of yourself because

the mirror distorts your perception.) Though a distorted perception of reality may be acceptable in certain environments, it's neither appropriate nor responsible during an Akashic Records reading, where the goal of the reader is to reveal the Truth.

2. **Use your current legal name when opening your Records.**

   Every name has a unique energetic vibration. Using the vibration of your current legal name is what allows you access to your Records. And using your full name—Suzette Joann Bailey, rather than Suzy Bailey, Suzy Jo Bailey, or Suzy J. Bailey—allows for a deeper, richer reading. When you change your name legally (as in the case of marriage or divorce, for example), you change your vibration in the Akashic Records, as well as the direction your life can take. So use the name that is on your legal documents, even if it's not the name you use every day. If there's any confusion about this, ask yourself: "How does the IRS know me?" This guideline also applies when you read the Akashic Records for others.

3. **Be responsible for your time in the Records.**

   Especially when you're first getting used to being in the Records, it's important to spend enough time during a reading to allow your consciousness to fully shift. This shift will allow you to get firmly "entrenched" in the Akashic field and receive information as clearly as possible. Between fifteen minutes and an hour in the Records is an appropriate amount of time to spend. Anything less than fifteen minutes will feel less like an Akashic Records reading and more like a quick-fix oracle in the realm of a yes-or-no question. Later in this chapter, we will discuss the kinds of questions that work best during Akashic readings and offer an explanation of why yes-or-no questions are not as effective as how-and-why questions.

4. **Ground yourself after each reading.**

    As you transition out of, or "close," the Akashic Records, your consciousness shifts back to your human perspective. To prevent yourself from feeling disoriented after this shift, do something to ground yourself: Drink a glass of water. Wash your face. Have a bite to eat. Go outside and hug a tree. Walk around barefoot—whatever works best for you and fits your immediate circumstances. The reason for grounding yourself is to bring your awareness back to the present moment and make yourself fully aware of your surroundings. Two grounding techniques that work well for me are taking my dog for a walk and taking out the trash. Both of these methods require me to let go of the reading and be present with what I am doing.

5. **When combining the Akashic Records with any other system, always honor both methods.**

    And conversely, if the guidelines and procedures for a particular system conflict with the guidelines for reading the Akashic Records, don't use the two systems together. Here's an example: You're considering opening your Records while partaking in Ritual Z, which requires you to eat hallucinogenic mushrooms. But you know that you must abstain from alcohol and drugs for twenty-four hours before opening your Records. Since Ritual Z's procedures conflict with these guidelines, practice these systems separately. In this way, you can honor each system's methods and keep each system pure and effective.

Guidelines for Reading the Akashic Records for Others

1. **Before opening a person's Records, obtain their permission.**

    Open someone's Records only when they ask you to do so. Always be aware that Akashic readings are "by invitation only," so don't tell people that they need readings or coerce them into consenting when they're uncomfortable with the idea. Know that it's up to each person to decide whether or not to have a reading. Even when it appears that a person's Soul or Higher Self is longing for a reading, if that human being cannot or will not ask for a reading, then the timing is not right—and doing a reading would not be right either.

2. **Maintain the strictest confidentiality.**

    If you are interested in doing Akashic readings for other people, you probably already possess a natural sensitivity to their needs—especially the need for privacy. So, of course, you will honor the confidential nature of this work and will not discuss other people's readings. As in all things, the Golden Rule applies here: Do unto others as you would have them do unto you. If you're ever on the receiving end of a reading, you will especially appreciate this guideline.

3. **Present all the information you get as positively, kindly, and respectfully as possible.**

    The goal of every reading is to dignify and elevate the person being read, to reveal that person's true self and potential. Gently and respectfully share everything that a person's Masters, Teachers, and Loved Ones reveal, even if it makes you uncomfortable, it seems insignificant, or it doesn't make sense to you. Sometimes the thing that you hold back from saying is exactly what a person most needs to hear.

4. Do not open the Records of individuals younger than eighteen years of age.

Each culture has its own definition of when a child becomes an adult. In the United States, adulthood is generally recognized as eighteen years of age. The Pathway Prayer Process honors the cultural norms of the United States because it is this system's place of origin. Until children reach the age of eighteen, they are the legal responsibility of their parents or guardians and are not allowed to make choices for themselves. Since having an Akashic Records reading requires individuals to take responsibility for their own actions (and karma), children must wait until they're eighteen to have a reading. This does not mean, however, that parents can't open their own Records and ask questions about raising their children. Valuable information is available regarding why our children are in our lives, how we can best support their growth, and what lessons we can learn from our relationships with them. (I am sometimes asked if it's okay to open the Records of a "mature" seventeen-and-a-half-year-old. My answer is always the same: If those children are truly mature, they'll understand why it's important to wait until they turn eighteen.)

Recommendations for the First Thirty Days

Once you make a conscious commitment to learn the Pathway Prayer Process, your initiation period begins, and you enter a "transitional thirty-day grace period." So if you simply open this book, read the prayer, and start to use it, you may not get the immediate results you desire. However, if you take the time to read the entire book and decide to work within its guidelines and ground rules, you will surely enter the zone of grace that will lend energetic support to your endeavor.

After you read the guidelines and ground rules, you may decide you're not ready just yet to open your Akashic Records. That's okay. The thirty-day transition begins when you decide to give the Records a fair try. You know what "fair try" means for you, and it's your decision, so you get to be the one who says what's fair. If something happens in your life that requires your full attention, and you can't work in the Records for a while, don't worry. Just let the Records go until you are ready to start anew. Your thirty-day grace period will also begin again. During that time, the Lords of the Records will gently guide you as you make your way in this exciting new spiritual realm.

During those early days, as you begin to read for others, the following guidelines will help ease your anxiety.

For Thirty Days after You Learn to Read the Akashic Records

1. ***Do* offer Akashic readings to others.**

    Once you learn to access the Akashic Records, the quickest way to get comfortable giving readings is to practice as much as you can. Therefore, it's permissible *during this thirty-day period only* to offer people readings instead of waiting to be asked. Tell people that you just learned to read the Records, and ask if you can practice on them. If they agree to have a reading, terrific. If they hesitate or say no, take that as your cue: Stop. Leave them alone. Ask somebody else.

2. ***Do not* collect money for your Akashic readings.**

    Offering free readings for the first thirty days will allow for the fact that you're still learning, and your readings may not be perfect. This approach will give you latitude to stretch and grow, and it will ease any "pressure to perform." When you do begin to charge for your readings, be sure to ask your Masters, Teachers, and Loved Ones what fee is appropriate for you.

3. **Do *not* mix your readings with other systems or disciplines.**
Before you start mixing your Akashic work with any other systems, it's important to know what the Records are as well as what they do. Otherwise, you may not be able to tell which practice is creating which result. (As I like to say, "Before you mix a drink, you need to know what's in each bottle.")

WHAT KINDS OF QUESTIONS WORK BEST IN THE AKASHIC RECORDS?

One of the most important keys to conducting an accurate and powerful reading is knowing what kinds of questions to ask. Some questions will yield lots of information from the Records, while others will yield little or no information—or they won't yield the *kind* of information you're seeking. Over the years, I have been asked and answered thousands of questions, so many that I created a resource to use when you are ready to dive deeper: *100+ Questions & Answers About the Akashic Records*.

So as you begin to formulate your questions, here are three basic guidelines to follow:

1. **Avoid questions that start with *when*.**
Time does not matter in the Records because the Records are eternal. They exist everywhere, all at once, and always in the here and now. Therefore, your Akashic Masters, Teachers, and Loved Ones are neither bound by, nor to, the parameters of earthly space and time. So asking them a

predictive question about when something will happen will not give you the answer you want, and you may even end up feeling frustrated, as in the following question posed by the fictional Mary Margaret.

Mary Margaret: *Masters, Teachers, and Loved Ones, when will I find the love of my life?*

Of course, the answer Mary Margaret wants and expects is something measurable and definitive, such as, "You will find the love of your life within the next three months." However, since the Masters, Teachers, and Loved Ones (MTLOs) don't deal in earthly time, they won't give her a measurable, definitive answer. Instead, they might respond like this:

MTLOs: *Mary Margaret, you will find the love of your life after you forgive your ex-husband and release him once and for all. On paper, you've been divorced for three years now, and your ex-husband has moved on and found someone else. However, in your mind and in your heart, you haven't moved on. You're still holding onto that relationship through your anger and resentment, and that is keeping you stuck. Please accept everyone concerned and move forward. The sooner you can do that, the sooner you'll be free, and the sooner you'll be able to find a new love and a relationship that nurtures and fulfills you.*

But Mary Margaret is not happy with that answer at all!

Mary Margaret: *What? No! That's not the answer I asked for! That's not what I want to hear! I didn't ask about me. I asked about the love of my life and when I'm going to find him. . . .*

You get the idea. Time-related, predictive questions don't work well in the Akashic Records, especially when the issue in question could take more than one lifetime to resolve!

2. **Avoid questions with yes-or-no responses.**
   Questions requiring yes-or-no answers don't work well in the Records either because the outcome is ultimately up to you; it's determined by your choices and life circumstances. Here is another example, this time with the fictional Thomas.

Thomas: *I was offered a new job this week. Should I take it?*

Thomas now expects a simple one-word answer: *yes* or *no*. However, the Masters, Teachers, and Loved Ones have a different answer in mind. It is based on their knowing that in order for Thomas to be truly satisfied, the decision must be *his,* not *theirs.* Thomas must look inside to determine who he is as well as what kind of work he likes and does best. Then, he must consider the advantages and disadvantages inherent in both his current job and the new prospect. Next, he must decide which job best suits his goals and needs. After carefully considering all those factors, Thomas will finally have his answer, and at that point, he won't need any outside help in knowing what to do. So instead of hearing *yes* or *no* from his Masters, Teachers, and Loved Ones, Thomas might hear something like this:

MTLOs: *Well . . . why are you considering this job in the first place, and what might happen if you take it? Let's explore the possibilities of the new job for a while, then weigh them against the realities of your current job. First, regarding the job you've been offered: What would be some of the advantages of taking it? What would be some of the drawbacks? How do the job requirements match your current abilities and interests? Are they in line with your current needs? Will they support your future goals? Now, let's look at your current job . . .*

That's a lot more words than *yes* or *no*. Again, though, you get the idea. Yes-or-no questions don't work well in the Records. They diminish people's power by putting the decision-making process—and ultimately, the outcome—in someone else's hands. But the Akashic Records *give* people power by helping them examine a situation, see what's true, and then decide for themselves what feels right. In other words, there are no *shoulds* in the Records. Your Masters, Teachers, and Loved Ones will broaden your perspective and will help you weigh your options, but they will not make your decisions for you or tell you what you should do. As always, they leave responsibility where it belongs—with you.

Our challenge as human beings on this planet is to live in the present moment as much as we possibly can. When we're focused on some point in the future or are letting someone else tell us how things should go, we're neither present in a particular moment nor responsible for ourselves. But when we seek the perspective of the Masters, Teachers, and Loved Ones, they help us empower ourselves to be who we need to be in any given moment. Providing Truth, information, and support is the role of the Akashic Records. So if you really need a time-related answer, there are oracles such as clairvoyants, card readers, and astrologers who can help. And if you need a yes-or-no answer, a pendulum works especially well.

3. **Stick with questions that answer *what*, *why*, or *how*.**

The questions that work best in the Records usually begin with *what*, *why*, or *how*. For example, instead of asking, "When will my soulmate appear?" or "Should I stay with my partner?" try one or more of the following questions:
- Why are my partner and I together?
- What are the possibilities for us as a couple?
- What are the advantages and/or disadvantages of us being together at this time?
- Our relationship is strained/broken/irreparable. What happened to make it so?
- What am I not seeing, and why am I not seeing it?
- How can I change my perspective and see what I need to see?
- What is my part in this relationship?
- What can I do right now to find peace, acceptance, and healing?

WHAT SHOULD I EXPECT WHEN I OPEN MY AKASHIC RECORDS FOR THE FIRST TIME?

No two people have the same experience when opening their Records for the first time, so it's best to go into your experience with as few expectations as possible. Now, having said that, let me tell you about a few things you *can* expect!

The first thing that will happen while you're accessing your Records is that while you speak the Opening Prayer, you'll shift out of your ordinary human consciousness and into the divine universal consciousness. When you open your Records for the first time, you may or may not sense this shift in any way. Rest assured, however, that by the time you've finished the prayer, the shift will have occurred. This shift will not be dramatic, and it will not involve strange or sensational phenomena: no talking in funny voices, no eyes rolling back in the head, no entity coming in and taking over, no leaving yourself in the process. It will just be you, as you always are, speaking as you always do. The only difference will be in *what* you say because you'll be receiving information from the Akashic field, which is a different energetic dimension.

At this point, you may be wondering if any "negative" energy or "dark" entities can enter your consciousness or attach to you while you're in the Akashic Records. My answer to you is *no*—unequivocally, unmistakably no. As you will come to understand when I explain the Prayer, you are calling upon *only* the forces of Light and are inviting *only* the Holy Spirit of God. So it is the power of that Divine Light that will uphold and protect you from anything that is not strictly of the Light. Will you feel the Light? Maybe, maybe not. But again, rest assured that you are being held firmly in its accelerated and rarified frequency, and you have absolutely nothing to fear.

WHAT KINDS OF INFORMATION WILL I GET, AND HOW WILL I GET IT?

When people access the Akashic Records, they get all kinds of information. Yet, in one important way, it's always the same: It always elevates the person being read. In the section about appropriate questions to ask, I explained the kinds of answers you will *not* get from the Records. I'd like to add to that here by saying that neither will you get information that makes fun of you, belittles you, or judges you in any way. If you begin to sense judgment while you're in the Records, know that it's coming from you, and ask the Masters, Teachers, and Loved

Ones for help in showing you your Soul's true essence as a divine spiritual being.

As to *how* you might get information, you may find that when you first begin opening your Records, you receive information in only one way. You may only see colors or hear words, for example. Yet after being in the Records repeatedly, your ability to hold steady in the Light will increase, and you can receive information in any of the following ways:

- **You may "hear" information in your head.** This may include words, phrases, or a longer narrative (which one of my students calls "streaming audio"). Sometimes people ask what the Masters, Teachers, and Loved Ones "sound like." As you might expect, they "sound" very different from one reading to the next—as unique, as a matter of fact, as the individual being read. So sometimes their tone is formal, and sometimes it's casual. Sometimes their tone is serious, and sometimes it's humorous. Sometimes they speak in metaphors, and sometimes they're very literal. And sometimes they use the Socratic method—answering your questions with even more questions until you arrive at an answer for yourself. Always, however, they are compassionate. They serve with objective nonjudgment while facilitating your Soul's growth and healing.
- **You may "see" things in your mind's eye.** You may see colors, auras, or energy fields; images, symbols, or shapes; or "streaming video" of a particular event.
- **You may experience various emotional or physical feelings in your body.** These may include tingling, excitement, heat, or cold, for example. If you experience a feeling that's uncomfortable, just acknowledge what it is. Know that it cannot harm

or affect you, and it will not stick around. Thank the Masters, Teachers, and Loved Ones for giving you the information in this way, let them know you've received the message, and ask them to make the feeling stop.

When people begin this work, I suggest they experiment going into their Records with the intention of describing their experiences first. This is very different from evaluation. Simply describe what's happening or what's not happening. As you put words to your experience, the energy moves. If you are on the right track, then more will be revealed. If not, it will dry up rather quickly, leaving you to explore a different avenue or come back at a different time. I also understand that many come to the Akasha with natural talents. Keep in mind that, while it's great to have this gift, it's even more important to be willing to practice. Keep your expectations low and practice every chance you get. Practice will empower you to become a wonderful Akashic Records Practitioner.

By now, you have a good overview of guidelines and ground rules for opening the Akashic Records, as well as some information about the ways in which you might receive information from them. Now, we will move ahead to chapter 3, which contains a thorough explanation of the Pathway Prayer Process to Access the Heart of the Akashic Records. It also contains more information about what to expect when you open your Records for the first time. But before you begin reading the chapter, please take a few moments to consider what you've read so far, and decide whether this work is for you.

If you decide that working in the Records will never be right for you, please pass this book to someone else who would like to explore the Records. If you would like to work in the Records someday but feel that this isn't the right time, then set the book aside until you're ready to begin again. If you feel ready to work in the Records right now, I invite you to continue reading with an open heart and mind. As I've mentioned, working in the Records is an entirely personal decision. Only you know what kinds of practices will best support your spiritual growth and authority and when you are ready for them. The Lords of the Records understand this perfectly, and they honor your decisions.

3

The Pathway Prayer Process

The Pathway Prayer Process to Access the Heart of the Akashic Records is a procedure that allows you to be in conscious relationship with the Akashic Records in order to develop your spiritual awareness. As its name suggests, it is a vibrational "pathway" constructed by the words and sounds of the Prayer. This Pathway Prayer serves as an energetic bridge, a direct route of access, to the Heart of the Akashic Records.

As you speak the Opening Prayer, the energetic vibrations from the sounds of its specific words and phrases construct a bridge of Light that allows you to safely shift from your ordinary human consciousness into the divine universal consciousness. Then later, as you speak the Closing Prayer, your consciousness shifts back until you are "your old self" again.

Since the day I received the Pathway Prayer from my Akashic Records, I have never been afraid. I have had no fear of exploring or testing the Prayer or the Pathway Prayer Process on myself or my Akashic students. I always have had, and continue to have, a deep commitment to share with others any spiritual resources that have been beneficial to me, my students, and my clients. I believe that the Pathway Prayer came to me because I have the willingness to take it as far as I can in order to see what good will come from it. I know that my personal combination of curiosity, willingness, and a desire to serve make me a likely candidate. I also know, however, that if I had declined the opportunity, the Prayer would have been given to someone else because now is the time in humanity's development for the Universal Heart to open and the Universal Soul to lead—through the open heart of each person on the planet—to the unification and elevation of all.

When you read the Pathway Prayer, you will note that its language is traditionally Christian. Since this might be a sensitive issue for some people, I'd like to take a moment to explain the words and their context. The Prayer came to me in the Midwestern United States, in the Western Hemisphere of the world. The words reflect the most familiar language and understandings of this region in order to make the Prayer as accessible as possible to the general population. "God" is a common identifying word for the Divine Presence in this part of the world. And when I use the words "Holy Spirit," I am referring to the Spirit of God, as opposed to any individualized personality or personification of the God Force.

In the next section, you will find an annotated version of the Pathway Prayer that you will use to access and read your own Records. The annotations explain not only the meaning of the Prayer, but what happens as you say each line. In the Appendix, you'll find the Prayer reprinted without notes. That is the version you can bookmark and use to open your own Records in the future. For now, though, it will be most useful for you to read the annotated version first so you can learn the process for reading your own Records. (In the next chapter, we will look at the

Prayer you will use to do Akashic readings for others. It varies only slightly from this Prayer.)

Once you have read and understood the Prayer, you will be ready to open your Records for the first time. You won't ask any questions at that time; you'll simply sit in the energy for several minutes, acclimate to the feeling, and observe. Then, after you close your Records, I'll guide you through an exercise, during which you'll open your Records again and ask a question.

UNDERSTANDING THE PATHWAY PRAYER PROCESS: READING FOR YOURSELF

The Pathway Prayer Process to Access the Heart of the Akashic Records Opening Prayer

When reading for yourself, say this part aloud:

1. And so we do acknowledge the Forces of Light,

2. Asking for guidance, direction, and courage to know the Truth

3. as it is revealed for our highest good and the highest good of

4. everyone connected to us.

In the first line of the Prayer, both your *finite being* (the person you are in this lifetime) and your *infinite being* (your eternal Soul) are calling forth and aligning with the higher realms of Light. In so doing, you are establishing a connection to the Akashic Records through a vertical pillar of Light. This connection begins about eighteen inches above your crown, at your eighth chakra. This chakra, which is also known as the Soul Chakra, is the point of interface between the Soul plane and the physical plane. As the Light passes through your eighth chakra and descends to your seventh, it starts to become denser and gather form. By the time the Light reaches your seventh chakra, its vibration is dense enough that you are able to discern it as the unique vibrational Record of your individual Soul.

In lines two through four, you are asking for three things: guidance, direction, and the courage to fearlessly and willingly receive the Truth (not predictions) to the best of your ability and for everyone's highest good.

5. Oh, Holy Spirit of God,

6. Protect me from all forms of self-centeredness,

7. and direct my attention to the work at hand.

Fear, self-importance, and self-seeking (seeking validation and approval to bolster a flailing self) are your greatest detractors in the Records. They magnetize distractions and diminish your ability to hold steady in the Light and receive information. As you speak lines five through seven, the Holy Spirit helps you shift your attention away from yourself and your performance, and helps you focus on the reading. Not allowing yourself to be distracted by personal concerns actually becomes the protection mentioned in line six because if your focus is appropriate while you're in the Records, there's no chance of falling prey to outside influences. You'll be immune to anything that is not of the Light as long as you remain in a mode of service to the person whose Records you are reading. (Right now, you are reading for yourself. In the future, however, you could be reading for someone else.)

Keeping your attention focused on the reading also keeps you grounded in the present, which holds you steady in the pillar of Light and allows the information and the reading to flow.

8. Help me to know myself in the Light of the Akashic Records,

9. To see myself through the eyes of the Lords of the Records,

10. And enable me to share the wisdom and compassion that the Masters, Teachers, and Loved Ones of me have for me.

As you say lines eight through ten aloud, you are asking the Holy Spirit to help you see yourself as you are seen, known, and loved in the Akashic Records. You are using the words "myself" and "me" because you are referring to yourself as who you are every day in the physical dimension.

It's important to have a clear idea of who you are dealing with as you navigate the Records. This is a good time in our process to examine who the Lords of the Records, Masters, Teachers, and Loved Ones are, as well as their roles and responsibilities within the Akasha.

The Lords of the Records

The Lords of the Records are a group of Light Beings who work at the universal level, rather than with individual Souls. Light Beings are nonphysical beings who are involved at every level of awareness. They invigorate and generate a higher quality of Light in every corner of our Universe. Over time, this higher quality of Light translates into an improved quality of life for all humans. It also affords greater potential for understanding the higher Truths about oneself and others.

The Lords of the Records are responsible for maintaining the integrity and incorruptibility of the Akashic Records. As such, they decide who may and may not access the Records. They also decide what information will be revealed during a particular reading. Once they make that decision, they give the information to the Masters, Teachers, and Loved Ones of the Soul who is seeking guidance. Or sometimes they withhold information if it wouldn't be beneficial or the timing isn't right. That's why we sometimes don't get answers when we ask particular questions. (If you've gotten this far in the book, the Lords of the Records have determined that now is the time for you to access the Akashic Records.)

The Masters

The Masters are also a group of Light Beings. Like the Lords of the Records, they have never been in physical bodies. But unlike the Lords, who work at the universal level, they work with individual Souls. Your particular Masters have been with you since your Soul's inception and are responsible for your Soul's ongoing growth and development. In other words, they are responsible for getting you on the path and keeping you there. At your Soul's inception, together with your Masters, you chose the plan for your Soul throughout time: "My Soul will learn these specific lessons as it becomes aware of itself." Based on the spiritual Truths your Soul chose to experience, your Masters will call upon certain Teachers and Loved Ones to support your mastery in various situations and lifetimes. So, depending on the notion you are working on at any given time, when you open your Records to discuss it, your Masters will call upon just the right Teachers and Loved Ones that are suited to help you best. Just as you can have more than one Master, a Master can have more than one Soul in its charge.

The Teachers

The Teachers may or may not have been in physical bodies before. Unlike your Masters, your Teachers are not with you throughout your Soul's existence. Instead, they are lesson-specific: Each one only stays with you for as long as it takes you to learn a particular lesson and integrate the consciousness of that Teacher—whether that's a certain period during a single lifetime or a span of several incarnations. Once you have learned the lesson and integrated the consciousness of that Teacher or Teachers, it will move on to work with other Souls.

If your Teachers ever were in physical form, they may have been "ordinary folks" when they lived on earth. Or they may have been "biggies," such as Jesus or Buddha or Mother Teresa. Either way, your Akashic Teachers prefer to remain unidentified because they don't want to foster your dependence upon them—or their earthly identities. As you'll read next, this holds true for the Loved Ones as well. Since the Akashic Records are meant to be a pathway to spiritual and emotional maturity, the job of your Masters, Teachers, and Loved Ones is to help you develop a reliance on the *divine essence and energy* of the Records, rather than on a particular being or identity.

The Loved Ones

The Loved Ones are people you knew in this lifetime but who are now deceased. Although they are committed to your Soul's growth and evolution, your Loved Ones are not necessarily connected to you on an emotional level. Instead, they may have been distant relatives or acquaintances who watched you from afar while they were alive but who, after they died, chose to actively support and serve you. Like your Teachers, your Loved Ones prefer not to be identified so you don't become dependent on them as the personalities you knew in this lifetime. However, they *will* reveal themselves during a reading if they feel like that will support you in the moment. Even when they do come forward, though, they never conduct the reading. It's more like they step forward to say hi, then step back again.

Every person has Akashic Loved Ones—even Souls whose earthly bodies died at birth or only lived for a very short time. In such cases, previously deceased members of that Soul's ancestral line—a grandparent, for example—will fill the role of that person's Loved One.

Now that we know who will be meeting us in the Records, let's return to the Prayer.

Read this part silently to yourself:

11. Help me to know (*your current legal name*) in the Light of the Akashic Records,

12. To see (*your current legal name*) through the eyes of the Lords of the Records,

13. And enable me to share the wisdom and compassion that the Masters, Teachers,

14. and Loved Ones of (*your current legal name*) have for me.

15. Help me to know (*your current legal name*) in the Light of the Akashic Records,

16. To see (*your current legal name*) through the eyes of the Lords of the Records,

17. And enable me to share the wisdom and compassion that the Masters, Teachers,

18. and Loved Ones of (*your current legal name*) have for me.

As you silently read lines eleven through eighteen to yourself, you are being moved into an expanded state of consciousness. This state is anchored in the physical dimension, yet can register the more subtle impressions and vibrations of the dimension of the Akashic Records. Also occurring simultaneously:

- The vibration of your current legal name calls up the Records of your Soul. Your Records are then brought forward by the Lords of the Records and are given to

your Masters, Teachers, and Loved Ones. They, in turn, "download" the specific information you will need for this particular reading.
- Energy from the Heart of the Akashic Records moves down through your crown and registers its vibration deep behind your heart center. Your heart center is your "receptor site" for the information you'll receive from the Records. When this energetic anchoring is complete, the shift in your consciousness will also be complete.

Announce the opening of the Records by saying this part aloud:

19. The Records are now open.

Your shift in consciousness is fully complete. You now have access to your Akashic Records and your Masters, Teachers, and Loved Ones.

Closing Prayer

When you are ready to end your session in the Records, say this part aloud:

20. I would like to thank the Masters, Teachers, and Loved Ones

21. for their love and compassion.

22. I would like to thank the Lords of the Akashic Records for their point of view.

23. And I would like to thank the Holy Spirit of Light for all knowledge and healing.

24. The Records are now closed. Amen.

25. The Records are now closed. Amen.

26. The Records are now closed. Amen.

Being granted access to the Akashic Records is both an honor and a privilege and should not be taken lightly. Of course, you will want to express gratitude to all the Light Beings who made your experience possible.

Just as it took some time for you to shift out of your ordinary state of consciousness, it takes some time to shift back again. This shift, or transition, is a journey of sorts; and every journey has a beginning, a middle, and an end. Saying line twenty-four signals the beginning of the shift, saying line twenty-five signals the middle, and saying line twenty-six signals the end.

Once you have closed the Records, don't forget to ground yourself in whatever way works best for you (see chapter 2 for some examples). As I mentioned earlier, this Prayer is reprinted in the Appendix so you can use it to open and close your own Records.

Pathway Prayer Process to Access the Heart of the Akashic Records When Reading for Yourself Opening Prayer

When reading for yourself, say this whole part aloud:

> And so we do acknowledge the Forces of Light,
> Asking for guidance, direction, and courage to know the Truth
> as it is revealed for our highest good and the highest good of
> everyone connected to us.

Oh, Holy Spirit of God,
Protect me from all forms of self-centeredness,
and direct my attention to the work at hand.
Help me to know myself in the Light of the Akashic Records,
To see myself through the eyes of the Lords of the Records,
And enable me to share the wisdom and compassion that the Masters, Teachers, and Loved Ones of me have for me.

Read this part silently to yourself:

Help me to know (*your current legal name*) in the Light of the Akashic Records,
To see (*your current legal name*) through the eyes of the Lords of the Records,
And enable me to share the wisdom and compassion that the Masters, Teachers, and Loved Ones of (*your current legal name*) have for me.
Help me to know (*your current legal name*) in the Light of the Akashic Records,
To see (*your current legal name*) through the eyes of the Lords of the Records,
And enable me to share the wisdom and compassion that the Masters, Teachers, and Loved Ones of (*your current legal name*) have for me.

Announce the opening of the Records by saying this part aloud:

The Records are now open.

Closing Prayer
Say this part aloud:

> I would like to thank the Masters, Teachers, and Loved Ones for their love and compassion.
> I would like to thank the Lords of the Akashic Records for their point of view.
> And I would like to thank the Holy Spirit of Light for all knowledge and healing.
> The Records are now closed. Amen.
> The Records are now closed. Amen.
> The Records are now closed. Amen.

(For a condensed version of the Pathway Prayer Process, see the Appendix.)

At this point, you may be wondering how angels, saints, spirit guides, and other Light Beings you may have heard about or experienced relate to the Akashic Records. Since the Akasha is the All That Is—the primary substance from which everything originates—Light Beings such as angels and saints exist within the Akasha. Yet they reside in, and are supported by, a different realm from the Akashic Records. Though their *energy* exists in the Akasha, these particular Light Beings are not directly accessible through the Akashic Records; this is because their work is different from the work of the Masters, Teachers, and Loved Ones.

As I said earlier, the role of the Masters, Teachers, and Loved Ones is to support us in taking personal responsibility for our lives. As we work in the Akashic Records, the power and energy of the Records move *through* us, then we take the information and clarity we receive and use it to take care of ourselves. So, in a sense, we work in the Records to learn to "parent" ourselves. Conversely, when we call upon angels, saints, and other Light Beings to ask for their help and protection, we hand the power and responsibility to them, and they do the caretaking for us. Whichever we choose to do, it's a win-win situation because what do you think supports the entire realm of the angels and all other Light Beings? That's right: the Akasha—the All That Is!

Angels, Saints, and Spirit Guides

In what ways do the angels, saints, and spirit guides differ from the Akashic Masters, Teachers, and Loved Ones? The angels are similar to the Akashic Masters in that both groups work directly with individuals. The difference between the two groups, however, is that, while the Akashic Masters do not have individual identities, the angels have very specific identities, personalities, and powers. So an individual can call upon a particular angel—such as Michael or Raphael or Ariel—and ask that angel to use its unique powers to help with a specific need. While anyone can ask the angels for help at any time, some people who are highly clairvoyant can access the angelic realm and have what we might call "two-way conversations" with the angels.

The saints function much like the Akashic Teachers. Whereas the Teachers may or may not have had physical bodies and are most often unidentifiable in the Records, all of the saints once lived on Earth and have specific identities and roles. In the same way that people seek the help of specific angels, they seek the help of specific saints.

Spirit guides are similar to angels in that they have specific roles, responsibilities, and even implements. They often have strong personalities that are communicated to us when we face certain challenges in life. Spirit guides and angels often escort us into the Records. As we move deeper into our practice, those who escorted us into this Realm naturally step back until eventually we no longer need their services. Compared to the Masters, Teachers, and Loved Ones—who work in a group without specific identities or ego needs—spirit guides and angels support us as individuals with particular opinions and points of view. While it is customary to develop personal attachments to your angels or spirit guides, it is energetically impossible to form an empowering relationship with them like you can with your amorphous, egoless Masters, Teachers, and Loved Ones. This is a significant distinction.

READING YOUR AKASHIC RECORDS FOR THE FIRST TIME

Now that you understand the Pathway Prayer Process, you are ready to open your Records. First, prepare yourself by finding a quiet place where you're sure you won't be interrupted. Next, get yourself centered and grounded. The best way to get centered and grounded when preparing to work in the Records is to use the Pillar of Light meditation. This particular meditation will bring you into a state of reasonable balance within yourself and into a solid state of balance within your environment.

When you finish the meditation, take a few deep breaths and begin to focus your attention on the work at hand. Read the Opening Prayer as instructed. Don't ask any questions immediately after you say, "The Records are now open." Instead, just sit for a while and notice what is happening. Since your first experience in the Records will be entirely new and unique, try not to judge it. Know that you'll have the perfect experience based on who you are and what you need in the moment. Remember that the Lords of the Records have known and loved you since your Soul was born. Therefore, trust that they have told your Masters, Teachers, and Loved Ones precisely the best way to welcome you to the Records. Describe what is, or is not, occurring. Think about it or write it down. Do not try to evaluate either the way you are receiving the guidance or the guidance you are receiving. Simply describe your experience.

After spending about five or ten minutes in your Records, read the Closing Prayer as instructed. You may want to ground yourself afterward. Then, take a little time to contemplate your experience and/or write down a few notes about it. (As I mentioned earlier, the reason for grounding yourself is to get refocused on the physical earth and in your everyday life so you are fully present to what is happening around you.)

THE DIFFERENCE BETWEEN THE AKASHIC RECORDS AND INTUITION

After accessing their Akashic Records for the first time, new students often have questions about the difference between receiving information in the Records and listening to one's intuition. Common questions include:

- Is there a difference between opening my Records to get information and asking my intuition for information?
- If there *is* a difference, what is it?
- Is one way better than the other?

The short answer is yes, there is a difference. You can experience it firsthand in the following exercise.

EXERCISE

The Akashic Records and Intuition

PART 1: ACCESS YOUR INTUITION

- Think of a question that's been on your mind a lot lately—something relevant and "alive" in your life right now. As you formulate your question, remember that asking how, what, or why will get

you a more complete answer than asking a yes-or-no question.
- Write your question on a clean sheet of paper, leaving plenty of room below it to record an answer.
- Now, access your intuition and ask your question. (If the word "intuition" intimidates you, then call it something else. Think of it as your Higher Self, your inner wisdom, your inner voice, your gut feeling—anything that enables you to "tune in" and receive an answer to your question.) Either write the answer as it comes to you, or get your answer first and write it later.

PART 2: ACCESS YOUR AKASHIC RECORDS

- Once the answer from your intuition feels complete, say the Pathway Prayer to access your Akashic Records. After you say, "The Records are now open," ask your Masters, Teachers, and Loved Ones the very same question you asked your intuition. Again, either write the answer as you receive it or get your answer first and write it later.
- When you finish writing, go back and compare both answers. Are they almost the same? Noticeably different? Does either answer surprise you? Why or why not?

After doing this exercise in class, my students shared some interesting stories. Some of them said they received similar answers from their intuition and their Records. Many more of them, however, said they got different answers—different, yet not conflicting. To help illustrate this point, here are the real-life answers Julie got each time she asked her question.

Julie: *When my husband, Adrian, first took up archery, I thought it was kind of cool. It's a sport that requires focus, precision, and skill, and it seemed like something he would be good at. Well, he did get good at it—very quickly. Soon, though, he wasn't satisfied with just shooting his arrows at paper bull's-eyes. He wanted to go hunting for deer. I was shocked, appalled, incredulous! How could he hunt such beautiful creatures? Who would want to kill Bambi, let alone cook him up and eat him? I felt so conflicted. I didn't want to discourage my husband, yet I "conscientiously objected" to his zeal over what I viewed as his senseless new passion.*

Adrian took his first hunting trip this weekend. As he drove away, I made myself feel better by telling myself that he wasn't skilled enough to get a deer on his first time out—well, darn if he didn't get one yesterday. So my question today was a no-brainer: I'm so uncomfortable with my husband's deer hunting. What is behind my discomfort?

As instructed, Julie wrote down her question. Then she asked her intuition for an answer, and here is what she got.

Julie's intuition: *The reason you're so uncomfortable with your husband's deer hunting is because you could never kill an animal for sport. You view animals as sacred creatures, each with its own place and purpose on this planet. How could anyone hide for hours in a stand of trees, just waiting for a deer to pass, and then take its life in an instant? Adrian says his motive was neither malicious nor selfish; he took the deer for its meat. And as he thanked the animal for giving its life,*

> *he promised he wouldn't waste it. He also believes he was helping to control the deer population so that hundreds of deer don't starve this winter. But as valid and justifiable as all of these reasons may be, killing a deer with a bow and arrow is just something you wouldn't do. Besides, you didn't eat venison before, and you're certainly not going to start now.*

After thanking her intuition, Julie opened her Akashic Records. Then, she asked the same question of her Masters, Teachers, and Loved Ones.

> Julie: *I'm so uncomfortable with my husband's deer hunting. What is behind my discomfort?*

As Julie sat and listened to her Masters, Teachers, and Loved Ones, they explained what was going on. And pardon the expression, but they hit the bull's-eye! Here is what they said.

> Julie's MTLOs: *Come on now, Julie. Don't kid yourself. You eat chicken, you eat turkey, you eat fish—you'd eat sushi every day if you could. Where do you think all of that meat comes from? And some of it killed much less humanely than the way in which your husband killed his deer. Your objection to Adrian's hunting isn't all about killing and eating animals. Let's look at your discomfort from a different perspective—not in the context of hunting, per se, but in the context of how hunting affects your relationship. What's been one of your biggest complaints lately?*

Julie silently answered that she and her husband hadn't been spending as much time together as she would like.

Julie's MTLOs: *Yes. You wish that you and your husband weren't so busy, and that you could see each other more often. And regarding Adrian, what is one of your biggest fears?*

Julie answered that her biggest fear of all is that something will happen to Adrian, and she will lose the love of her life.

Julie's MTLOs: *Yes, that's the biggie . . . that you will lose the love of your life. Now can you see what's behind your discomfort? You feel that Adrian has so many hobbies and interests that already take him away from you, and now he's found yet another one to lose himself in. Not only will deer hunting take him away from you for long stretches at a time, it could also put him in harm's way, so this is kicking up your fears. What if he has a car accident while he's driving all that distance? What if he falls out of a tree stand and badly hurts himself? What if no one finds him, and he doesn't have his phone? What if another hunter shoots him with an arrow and maims him—or worse? Do you see it, Julie? Your discomfort has so little to do with the deer and so much more to do with your fear. You don't want to lose your "dear" Adrian, not even for a weekend. You don't want to waste time away from each other, especially on a "senseless new passion" that could threaten your husband's safety.*

And speaking of senseless new passions: This man supports you, Julie. In every way possible, he's your biggest fan and cheerleader. He's behind you in all of your interests and hobbies, even when they make him uncomfortable. So why not support him the way he supports you? You don't always have to agree with what

> *he's doing. But don't make him feel bad about this new interest because it's really not about the d-e-e-r as much as it is about the d-e-a-r. Share with your husband your concerns about his safety, and make him promise to keep his cell phone in his pocket—fully charged. And in addition to sharing your concerns, acknowledge the truth behind it all. You love him dearly, and you love your time together, and you miss him when he is away. But by now, you also know this: No hobby or passion that either of you has will ever overshadow your passion for each other. Especially if you're both happy as individuals, you'll be a very happy couple. After all that you two have gone through in order to be together, nobody's going anywhere, and that is the truth. Just know it and relax.*

So there you have them: Two very clear examples of the answers Julie got from her intuition and the Records. Notice how her second answer didn't conflict with the first. It just addressed the situation from a different perspective and filled in more of the details. While Julie's intuition answered the question from a narrower and more immediate perspective, the answer she got from her Records was from a broader and more "historical" context. (Had it been necessary, that historical context could have been another lifetime. For this particular answer, however, the historical context was a few decades.)

Let's look at the two methods separately, starting with intuition. Intuitive information is inherent within the self. It lives within the internal divine spark. It's you making contact with that spark within yourself, and the answers and information that you receive relate to what you're experiencing or feeling in a particular moment. Since you are only able to view things from your limited human perspective, what you receive is in the here and now—in this moment and in this lifetime. So the answers you get solve immediate problems or help you understand those "gut feelings" or thoughts that come to you like "lightning bolts out of the blue." But depending on how strongly you rely on your intuition, those answers can be unclear and erratic at times—or even nonexistent. And when they do exist, you may not know where they came from, so they won't necessarily effect lasting changes based on a larger knowing.

Still, there's a very important place for intuition. It's your intuition that compels you to *turn here* to avoid an accident or traffic jam. Or it says, *Don't leave home just yet,* so you can catch an important phone call. Or sometimes you have a gut feeling that says, *Look sharp! This needs your attention now!* and it helps you avoid a person or a situation that's not for your highest good.

Now, let's look at the Records. Akashic wisdom comes from outside of, or beyond, the self. It's you tapping into divine consciousness, so the answers and information you get are from a perspective that spans the Universe and covers every lifetime your Soul has ever lived. So when you get an intuitive "hit" about something whose reason may not be clear—or alternatively, if you don't get an intuitive hit at all—you can access your Records for clarity. When you do, your Masters, Teachers, and Loved Ones will provide the information that will help you wrap your head around the issue or question and see it from different angles. And with that new information and perspective, you'll be able to shift your thinking and handle things more effectively and, in many cases, change them dramatically and for good.

One way to think about intuition and the Records is to imagine that you're an actor on a stage. When you're using your intuition, you're standing in the beam of a single, focused spotlight. Though the beam illuminates you in your current lifetime, it doesn't light up the rest of the stage (also known as all the lifetimes your Soul has lived). However, when you access your Akashic Records, the

"Divine Director" flips a switch and sheds Light on what's all around you. Suddenly, you can see so much more! You can see who else is involved in a particular "scene" (karmic issue) and how their words and actions have been affecting you—both in this current lifetime and in others, if applicable. In that moment of illumination, you're then free to decide if you'd like to change the scene by changing your next lines and actions.

Just as the Akashic realm supports angels, saints, and other Light Beings who have their own roles and purposes, the Akashic Records support your intuition, which also has its own role and purpose. Put another way, if the Akashic Records were an ocean of information, your intuitive inklings would be like single drops of water from that deep, wide ocean—coming from and containing the same contents as the ocean, yet much smaller in size and scope.

COMMON QUESTIONS AND CONCERNS ABOUT THE AKASHIC RECORDS

When people first start working in the Akashic Records, they sometimes have doubts about themselves as well as the process. "Can it really be this simple?" they ask. "How can I be sure I'm in the Records? Do I even have a right to be in the Records? Am I worthy enough? Gifted enough? Intuitive enough? Does the information I get really come from the Masters, Teachers, and Loved Ones . . . or is it me just making stuff up?" Let's take a look at some of those questions one at a time.

Can it really be this simple?

Absolutely! Your part of the process—saying the Pathway Prayer with conscious and deliberate intent—really is that simple. But don't forget that accessing the Akashic Records is not a solo endeavor. It involves you, the Forces of Light, the Holy Spirit of the God Force, the Lords of the Records, and the Masters, Teachers, and Loved Ones. When you show up and do your part, all of these Light Beings show up too. And they literally move heaven and earth to help you shift your consciousness and access the Akashic Records. So your willingness and sincere desire for guidance, backed by a host of heavenly helpers, are your assurance that once you say, "The Records are now open," you will be in the Records every time. It really is that simple.

Do I have a right to be in the Records? Am I worthy enough?

Again, the answers are *yes* and *yes*. Every person on this planet has a right to access the Records because every person is a sacred child of God whose name is written in God's Book of Life—the Akashic Records. However, not every person has an interest or a desire to access the Akashic Records. As I mentioned earlier, if you were drawn to this book—and now, if you have read this far—it's because the Lords of the Records called you "collect, long-distance" and you accepted the charge, so consider it your engraved invitation.

Am I gifted or intuitive enough?

The information you receive from the Records comes from a higher spiritual consciousness that is *beyond* and *greater than* your intuition, so it doesn't really matter if you consider yourself intuitive or not. This is not to say that after you've been working in the Records for a time, your intuition won't get a lot stronger. It usually does since working in the Records helps you strengthen your connection to the Light, which increases your receptivity to spiritual guidance both in and out of the Records. It *is* to say that intuitive ability or a particular gift is not a prerequisite for working in the Records, nor will it necessarily make you a stronger reader. What *will* make you a stronger reader is your ability to get yourself as far out of the way as possible so you can place all of your attention on the reading and the guidance you are receiving. When you can let that guidance flow through you without impediment, that will be the best gift you can possibly give or have.

RECEIVING THE HELP OF YOUR MASTERS, TEACHERS, AND LOVED ONES

If you've said the Pathway Prayer with conscious and deliberate intent, you're in the Records. If you've gotten yourself out of the way and are getting loving guidance rather than personal thoughts or judgments, you're getting your information from the Records. It really is that simple, but just in case you need more reassurance, here are some questions you can ask your Masters, Teachers, and Loved Ones right now. Say the Pathway Prayer to open your Akashic Records, then ask these questions one at a time:

- What would help me be more receptive to the Akashic Records?
- What would help me be more receptive to my Masters, Teachers, and Loved Ones?
- What is currently blocking my receptivity, and how can it be released?
- How do I make peace and accept who I am at a deep level?

Again, you can write your answers as you receive them, or you can get your answers first and write them later. Then when you're finished writing, you can close your Records right away, or you can leave them open and do the following meditation to strengthen your experience of being in your Akashic Records. As you did for the Pillar of Light meditation, find yourself a comfortable chair in a quiet room. Seat yourself squarely with your back straight and your feet on the floor, and place your hands palms-up in your lap or on the arms of the chair.

Then, read through the following meditation at a pace that feels comfortable to you.

MEDITATION

Ask your Masters, Teachers, and Loved Ones to help you have the experience of being in your own Akashic Records. As you enter your Records, begin to scan the space around you... left to right, then right to left... top to bottom, then bottom to top. Make a slight movement with your physical body to get a sense of the Body of Light that surrounds you in your Records.

As you sit in your Records, register the presence of your Masters, Teachers, and Loved Ones. Sometimes their presence is a feeling, such as love or peace or stillness. Sometimes it's a sensation of warmth or softness. Sometimes it's a quality of illuminating Light. And sometimes it's a quality of support, which can be either strong or subtle.

Your awareness of your own self in your Records opens a new dimension and expands the space so there's plenty of room for you. Take some time to scan this dimension: Travel in through the crown of your head and move down... past your third eye... past your throat... and all the way down to your heart.

While you are scanning your physical body, the Light of the Akasha is moving through you. It extends from your crown to your root so it can serve as a force field that holds the energy in place.

Though the Akasha fills your entire physical body, its primary region is between your crown and your heart. Place yourself at your crown and look down to the floor of your heart center. It is a clear lake—a mirrored platform—the Akasha's anchoring point within you. As the Light of the Akasha makes contact with this platform, it becomes the gateway to your inner realms. The Light of your individual Soul bounces off this platform and travels back up through the pillar of Light. See your Light being intensified and strengthened by the Light of the Akasha.

It holds your throat chakra, but does not interfere with it or invade it. The Light is available but not invasive. As it holds your throat chakra, it serves as an infinite resource to encourage the verbal expression of your Soul into the world.

The stream of Light then continues behind your third eye and holds it and supports it. If this center of your body is fatigued, it can rest in the Light of the Akasha for support.

Take a few moments right now to ask your Masters, Teachers, and Loved Ones for any guidance they can offer for your work. This is an opportunity to develop your conscious partnership with your Masters, Teachers, and Loved Ones. If you have any questions for them at this time, you can ask those questions now.

If you feel that your view is dim, or you sense nothing coming to you, adjust your posture and put your shoulders back to open up your heart center and allow the Light to move deeper into that space.

As you prepare to close your Records, know that a pathway has been established and you have cleared your inner pillar of Light. You, as an agent and instrument of the Akashic Records, are clear, and you now have this infinite resource available to support you in your work.

Now, bring your attention back to this moment and this book, and close your Akashic Records.

DIFFERENT USES FOR THE AKASHIC RECORDS

There are many valuable ways in which people use the Records to benefit their lives. Some ways work particularly well for some people, while other ways don't work so well, if at all. The following examples provide some ideas for how you might work in the Records. Don't forget that until your transitional thirty-day grace period ends, it's not helpful to mix your Akashic readings with other systems or disciplines.

Reading for Individuals

As you know, you can read your own Akashic Records or the Records of other people. When opening another person's Records, you must have their consent. Use that person's current legal name as described under Guideline 2 (on page 51), and use the version of the Pathway Prayer provided in chapter 4.

Reading the Records of Animals or Pets

Occasionally, when a person works with animals for a living or has a strong affinity for them, that person can read animals' Records. If reading the Records of animals isn't for you, no problem. Read on to learn about several other ways you can work in the Records.

Reading the Records of an animal or a pet can yield helpful information about its temperament, needs, or a particular condition or diagnosis. But how do you get permission to read the animal's Records? Just ask, and it will tell you! Sit with the animal for a moment and tell it what you'd like to do. If the animal doesn't want to have its Records read, it might turn away from you or leave the room, or it might close its eyes. If it agrees to grant permission, however, it might look into your eyes, move closer, or sit near you or on your lap. If the animal is not nearby, its owner can give you permission to open its Records. If the animal has papers that state a registered name—Harold Jamison Trotter, for example—use that name to open its Records. However, if the animal doesn't have formal papers, then use its "go by" name, which might be Sweetie Pie, Max, or "the raccoon in my backyard." The Records do not address the transition from one species to another.

Reading the Records of a Home

If you have the permission of the person whose name is on the mortgage or lease, you may read the Records of that home to learn about its history, its purpose, and its energy. In the case of a home that's for sale, if the owner has placed it on the market and has signed a contract with a realtor, that owner is essentially saying, "This home is open for viewing on every level." Therefore, you may open the home's Akashic Records without obtaining permission. However, if the listing has expired or the home has been sold to a new owner, "public viewing" is no longer possible, and you must once again obtain the owner's permission to open the Records of that home. When opening the Records of a home, use its full address, including street, city or town, state, and postal code.

While it would make sense to most of us that an animal would have a "listing" in the Akashic Records because it has an obvious life force, it may be more challenging to read the Records of a home, which seems inert and lifeless by comparison. Every home *does* have its own energy and presence, however, which feels more like the energy of an area of land rather than the energy of a human or animal. Even so, every home's energy can be read and deciphered in the Akashic Records.

If you open the Records of a home, you might be able to detect some of its ideals, potentials, and probabilities. You also might get an idea of how that home is able to support its inhabitants and what it cannot accommodate. However, if you can't seem to read a home's Akashic Records, don't worry. Reading the Records of a home is actually secondary to asking about that home in its owner's Records.

Reading the Records of Public Monuments, Buildings, Parks, Cities, Towns, or Areas of Land

Information about objects, buildings, or places with publicly registered names (the Washington Monument; Stonehenge; the

Sistine Chapel; Mount St. Helens; Galena, Illinois; Everglades National Park; Arapaho National Forest) may be freely accessed in the Records. One of my students often wondered why she repeatedly visited, and felt so at home in, the town of Banff. After opening the Akashic Records of Banff in Alberta, Canada, she learned that she had lived a past life there that was filled with love and purpose. Because of that information, her next trip to Banff was even more special than all of the previous ones.

Reading the Records of a Company or Department Within a Company

If you own a business, opening its Akashic Records can yield information on how to choose and support your employees, how to make your working environment the best it can be, and what actions would be most beneficial for your company at a particular time. To open your company's Records, use its publicly registered name.

If you don't own a company but are the official head of one of its departments, you may open the Records of that department only. Use the name of both the company and your specific department—for example, the billing department of the Midwest Regional Sales office of GreenGrow International in Deerfield, Illinois.

Reading the Records of a Patient or Client

Some people who do energy work like to open the Records of specific clients to request the best ways to assist them. As always, practitioners must have each client's permission and current legal name before opening their Records. As an alternative, when getting permission is not possible, practitioners can open their own Records and ask how to best support a specific client, or clients. This same thing can be done by teachers, employers, or group leaders who are planning a class or meeting and would like to make the experience most effective.

Using the Records to Create

Some people enjoy opening their Records before or during a creative undertaking. For example, some people use the Records to write poems, books, or music. Others sculpt, draw, or paint. Still others dance. This method of using the Records varies according to individual needs and personalities. For example, it's difficult for some people to stay in the Records for extended periods of time, so for them, it's easier to open the Records, receive inspiration and guidance, close the Records, then create. For others, it's more advantageous to open the Records, ask for help and inspiration, then hang on for the ride!

Using the Records to Learn

Some people like to use the Records to learn about things at deeper levels. For example, students who want to truly understand a sacred or complicated text will read it with their Records open. This can be quite illuminating. Reading with your Masters, Teachers, and Loved Ones is like reading a book in which someone has highlighted the key concepts and written great notes in the margins—all for your edification!

It's also fun to study a painting, attend a religious service, or listen to music with your Records open. Just make sure that the music is something mellow or soothing rather than jarring. Also, remember to close your Records when you're finished studying or listening.

Learning to work in the Records is an exploration of possibilities. I encourage you to try reading the Records of a variety of people, places, and things in order to discover what works best for you. Try not to compare your experiences to those of other Akashic readers since each individual has different strengths and interests when working in the Records.

Now that you've read about several ways people use the Records, it's time to ask your Masters, Teachers, and Loved Ones which method, or methods, could work best for you. After opening your Records, here are some questions you can ask:

- What is the best way (or ways) for me to use the Pathway Prayer Process at this time?
- What are my unique gifts, talents, and abilities, and what are the best ways for me to use them in the Records?

Take a moment to consider your ordinary human self. You are the person you are for many good reasons. Your gifts, talents, and abilities, as well as ways for you to employ the Pathway Prayer Process, can be revealed through daily activities and a session in your Records. They are not secrets kept from you. It may just be that you minimize your natural gifts or think they are "no big deal." Life loves us, and one result of that love is that we are often naturally drawn to areas of human living wherein we excel. What are your interests and desires? Continue to explore this topic in your Records, and you will receive the guidance you deserve and need. Take the answers you receive to heart and incorporate them into your personal work with the Akashic Records and your life.

4

Reading the Akashic Records for Others

Sometimes we humans, with our limited perspectives, forget the Truth of who we are. We forget that despite what we *think* we see when we view ourselves in the mirror, in truth, we're eternal beings of Light whose essence is wholeness and wellness and goodness.

When you read other people's Akashic Records, you are in the unique and wonderful position of reminding them of who they are, letting them glimpse themselves as they are seen, known, and loved by God and their Masters, Teachers, and Loved Ones. When people begin to see the Light in themselves—and in others as well—they are able to let go of long-held beliefs and perceptions and replace them with forgiveness and healing.

As you may have already inferred, if you choose to read other people's Records, your experiences will be different every time. Not only will you get different information for each person, the ways in which you'll *receive* and *deliver* the information will be different every time as well. That's because an individual's Masters, Teachers, and Loved Ones know precisely what to say and how to say it in order for that person to best receive it. So if "Jane" is very visual, for example, her Masters, Teachers, and Loved Ones might show you an image or a scene that you can describe to her. That image or scene may or may not make sense to you, but don't be surprised if Jane says, "I get it! Yes! This all makes perfect sense." The important things for you to remember in this instance are to not judge the information and to deliver it in the way you receive it. Simply describe with words whatever the answer to the question seems to be. As you find words to share with the person, the energy will move, and you will receive more information. Conversely, if you are heading in a direction that is not helpful, it will evaporate. Knowing the difference comes with practice. No matter how you receive information—whether hearing, visioning, or another sense of knowing—all respond equally well to being described. Once you describe your experience, the other person will then be free to decide what it means and how to use it.

In some cases—especially if the information you're sharing during a reading is sensitive or uncomfortable—you may find that one or both of you begin to put up some form of resistance. That's okay. It's only fear talking, and it's bound to happen sometimes. (That's why we ask for "courage to know the Truth" in the Opening Prayer.) The first thing you both need to remember is that the Masters, Teachers, and Loved Ones are loving Beings of Light who only speak the Truth and whose only task during an Akashic Record reading is to support a Soul's growth and enlightenment. That said, you can ask the person's Masters, Teachers, and Loved Ones to help both you and the other person feel safe so you are free to deliver—and they are free to accept—the information and guidance you're receiving. It is perfectly appropriate to pause during a reading and silently say the Opening Prayer again to release any fear and uncertainty and strengthen your connection to the Light. It's also appropriate to pour both of you some water or take a few deep breaths together in order to relax any physical or emotional tension you're feeling. Whatever you decide to do, the purpose of this brief pause is to interrupt the energetic pattern of fear and transform it into one of safety and comfort.

When opening the Records of another person, you'll use the Pathway Prayer Process, yet you'll read the Prayer slightly differently, and the process will change a bit in order to include the other person. I'll explain these differences in the annotated Prayer that follows. You'll find the Prayer without annotations in the Appendix so you can use it to read for other people.

UNDERSTANDING THE PATHWAY PRAYER PROCESS: READING FOR OTHERS

The Pathway Prayer Process to Access the Heart of the Akashic Records for Others Opening Prayer

When reading for someone else, say this part aloud:

1. And so we do acknowledge the Forces of Light,

2. Asking for guidance, direction, and courage to know the Truth

3. as it is revealed for our highest good and the highest good of

4. everyone connected to us.

In the first line of the Prayer, you are calling forth and aligning with the higher realms of Light on behalf of yourself and the other person. As you acknowledge the Forces of Light, you (the reader) are establishing a connection to the Akashic Records through a vertical pillar of Light, in the same way you do when you are reading for yourself.

In lines two through four, you are asking for the same three things you ask for when reading for yourself—guidance, direction, and the courage to fearlessly and willingly receive the Truth (not predictions) to the best of your ability and for the highest good of all. The difference is that you are now asking for these things on behalf of yourself and the person for whom you are reading.

Say this part aloud:

5. Oh, Holy Spirit of God,

Read this part silently to yourself:

6. Protect me from all forms of self-centeredness,

7. and direct my attention to the work at hand.

Lines five through seven are read differently when you're reading for another person. Whether reading for yourself or another, always read line five aloud. However, when you're reading for someone else, read lines six and seven silently to yourself. This brief, silent prayer is only meant to be "heard" by your Masters, Teachers, and Loved Ones. It's a request that they'll keep you immune from anything that is not of the Light, and that they'll keep you in a mode of service to the person for whom you are reading. It also will allow the information and the reading to flow more smoothly and effectively.

Read this part aloud one time:

8. Help me to know *(the person's first name or nickname)* in the Light of the Akashic Records,

9. To see *(the person's first name or nickname)* through the eyes of the Lords of the Records,

10. And enable me to share the wisdom and compassion that the Masters, Teachers, and Loved Ones of *(the person's first name or nickname)* have for *(them)*.

In lines one through seven, you began establishing a vertical pillar of Light to connect you to the Akashic Records. Now, as you say lines eight through ten aloud, you are establishing a horizontal connection between yourself and the other person so the two of you are held and protected in a kind of bubble, or cocoon, of Light. The horizontal connection is established as the Light streams down from the Heart of the Akashic Records to your eighth chakra, then down through your crown, and out to the other person through your heart center.

You use the person's first name or nickname as you say lines eight through ten because you're referring to the person as who they are every day in the physical dimension. This name is also what the person calls themselves every day, so it's comfortable and familiar and not jarring to hear aloud. (This is especially important if a person is feeling anxious about the reading. Hearing their familiar name can help them relax.)

Read this part silently to yourself:

11. Help me to know *(the person's current legal name)* in the Light of the Akashic Records,

12. To see *(the person's current legal name)* through the eyes of the Lords of the Records,

13. And enable me to share the wisdom and compassion that the Masters, Teachers,

14. and Loved Ones of *(the person's current legal name)* have for *(him, her, or them).*

15. Help me to know *(the person's current legal name)* in the Light of the Akashic Records,

16. To see *(the person's current legal name)* through the eyes of the Lords of the Records,

17. And enable me to share the wisdom and compassion that the Masters, Teachers,

18. and Loved Ones of *(the person's current legal name)* have for *(him, her, or them).*

As you read lines eleven through eighteen silently to yourself, you are allowing yourself to be moved into an expanded state of consciousness. This state is anchored in the physical dimension yet can register the more subtle impressions and vibrations of the dimension of the Akashic Records. These things are also occurring simultaneously:

- The vibration of the person's current legal name calls up the Records of their Soul. Those Records are then brought forward by the Lords of the Records and are given to the person's Masters, Teachers, and Loved Ones. They, in turn, "download" the information that you will share with the person during this particular reading.
- Just as when you are reading for yourself, energy from the Heart of the Akashic Records moves down through your crown and registers its vibration deep behind your heart center. Your heart center is your "receptor site"

for the information you'll receive from the Records, be it for yourself or someone else. When this energetic anchoring is complete, the shift in your consciousness will also be complete.

Announce the opening of the Records by saying this part aloud:

19. The Records are now open.

Your shift in consciousness is fully complete. You now have access to the person's Akashic Records and their Masters, Teachers, and Loved Ones.

Closing Prayer

When you are ready to end your session in the Akashic Records, say this part aloud:

20. I would like to thank the Masters, Teachers, and Loved Ones

21. for their love and compassion.

22. I would like to thank the Lords of the Akashic Records for their point of view.

23. And I would like to thank the Holy Spirit of Light for all knowledge and healing.

24. The Records are now closed. Amen.

25. The Records are now closed. Amen.

26. The Records are now closed. Amen.

Being granted access to this person's Akashic Records was both an honor and a privilege; of course you will want to express gratitude to all the Light Beings who made the experience possible.

Just as it took some time for you to shift out of your ordinary state of consciousness, it takes some time to shift back again. This shift, or transition, is a journey of sorts, and every journey has a beginning, a middle, and an end. Saying line twenty-four signals the beginning of the shift, saying line twenty-five signals the middle, and saying line twenty-six signals the end.

TIPS ON READING FOR OTHERS

Remember, no one should be coerced into an Akashic Record reading. If you are invited to give a reading, however, here are some things to know or do in order to make that reading—and every reading—the best it can be.

Before . . .

- If you'll be conducting your readings in person, create a quiet space in your home or office where you and your clients will feel safe and comfortable. Make sure you will not be interrupted by colleagues, family members, pets, or other distractions. If you're not sure what kind of environment will best support your readings, here's a question you can ask in your Records: "How can I establish and maintain an environment of safety for working in the Records?"
- If you'll be conducting your readings by phone, make sure your phone battery is fully charged, and set up any recording equipment in advance. (Some Akashic readers like to record their sessions, then send a tape or digital file to their clients. Whether to record or not is entirely up to you.)

- Zoom and other video recording methods have become increasingly popular. I like to use this method. Always remind the client that the reading is the experience, and the recording is something different. They are free to do what they wish with it.
- If you will be charging a fee for a reading, make sure the payment is handled in advance so, at the appointed time, you can place all of your energy and attention on the reading and the person being read.
- As a way to ensure that your readings are focused and the information flows smoothly, ask your clients to prepare their questions in advance. (They don't have to supply you with their questions in advance; they just have to prepare them for themselves.) If they ask you what kinds of questions work best, explain that *how*, *what*, and *why* questions yield the most information, and time-related, predictive questions or ones requiring yes-or-no answers yield the least information, if any.
- Remind yourself that the goals of every reading are to dignify and elevate the person being read, to reveal that person's true self and potential as viewed in the Akashic Records, and to provide clarity, direction, and healing.

During . . .

- Doing readings for other people is a privilege that comes with responsibility. Especially when you're reading for someone you know, use the opportunity to support the person and not sabotage, judge, or harm. (In other words, it doesn't matter what you think of your sister's boyfriend. Keep your thoughts and opinions to yourself, and deliver only the information that your sister's Masters, Teachers, and Loved Ones provide.) Being able to tell the difference between your personal feelings and the Records is a skill that you will develop with practice. However, one of the clearest indicators that you're tangled up in your own stuff is insisting that a person do what *you* suggest—and then becoming angry if they resist. Another indicator is when you take your focus off the person and begin sharing information about yourself and how you managed a similar situation. The moment a reading becomes about you in any way, you have slipped out of the Records. If this happens, just pause and silently reread the Opening Prayer. This will remedy the situation, and you'll be able to proceed with the reading.

- If a person begins asking questions about other people—perhaps wanting to know their thoughts and motivations or how to persuade them to behave a certain way—pause and remind the person that you are in the Records of *their individual Soul*. Therefore, if "Trixie" wants information about "Trudy," the only information you will get will be information relevant to *Trixie's part* in her relationship with Trudy.
- If you begin to feel like you've slipped out of the Records at any point—or like you never gained full access even though you said the Prayer correctly—silently ask the Masters, Teachers, and Loved Ones for support. Or, as I mentioned earlier, you can reread the Opening Prayer to yourself as a way to redirect your focus and strengthen your connection to the Light.
- As I also mentioned earlier, while you're reading for another person, the two of you are being held together in a protective "cocoon" of Light. So it wouldn't be

unusual for you to occasionally feel an energetic charge if the person gets emotional. Don't worry if this happens. Since you'll be viewing the situation from the perspective of the Records, you'll know right away that you are not meant to experience or hold on to those feelings and emotions. You are merely meant to understand them so you can support the person in processing and releasing them. By the time you say the Closing Prayer, the emotional charge will be gone, as will your energetic connection to the person. You will never take on that person's issues or walk away with the energetic effects those issues generate.

Pathway Prayer Process to Access the Heart of the Akashic Records for Others Opening Prayer

When reading for someone else, say this part aloud:

And so we do acknowledge the Forces of Light,
Asking for guidance, direction, and courage to know the Truth as it is revealed for our highest good and the highest good of everyone connected to us.

Say this part aloud:

Oh, Holy Spirit of God,

Read this part silently to yourself:

Protect me from all forms of self-centeredness, and direct my attention to the work at hand.

Read this part out loud one time:

Help me to know *(the person's first name or nickname)* in the Light of the Akashic Records,
To see *(the person's first name or nickname)* through the eyes of the Lords of the Records,
And enable me to share the wisdom and compassion that the Masters, Teachers,
and Loved Ones of *(the person's first name or nickname)* have for *(him, her, or them)*.

Read this part silently to yourself:

Help me to know *(the person's current legal name)* in the Light of the Akashic Records,
To see *(the person's current legal name)* through the eyes of the Lords of the Records,
And enable me to share the wisdom and compassion that the Masters, Teachers,
and Loved Ones of *(the person's current legal name)* have for *(them)*.
Help me to know *(the person's current legal name)* in the Light of the Akashic Records,
To see *(the person's current legal name)* through the eyes of the Lords of the Records,
And enable me to share the wisdom and compassion that the Masters, Teachers,
and Loved Ones of *(the person's current legal name)* have for *(him, her, or them)*.

Announce the opening of the Records by saying this part aloud:

The Records are now open.

Closing Prayer
Say this part aloud:

> I would like to thank the Masters, Teachers, and Loved Ones for their love and compassion.
> I would like to thank the Lords of the Akashic Records for their point of view.
> And I would like to thank the Holy Spirit of Light for all knowledge and healing.
> The Records are now closed. Amen.
> The Records are now closed. Amen.
> The Records are now closed. Amen.

After . . .

- Sometimes you may feel like you're still receiving information, even after you've finished a reading. That's because even though you "turned off the tap" when you closed the person's Records, there's a bit of energy and information still left in the energy pipeline. Repeat the Closing Prayer aloud, and the information will stop completely.
- If you find yourself thinking or worrying about a person long after you've finished a reading, repeat the Closing Prayer aloud to put your mind at ease.

DEVELOPING AN "ALTITUDE OF CONSCIOUSNESS"

While giving Akashic readings for others, your goal is to fall in love with each and every Soul! This requires you to develop an "altitude of consciousness" that allows you to view the person sitting before you through the higher and broader perspective of the Masters, Teachers, and Loved Ones. In other words, if you keep looking for and following the Light as you receive information about the person, the Light will continue to strengthen and expand as it moves you from one Truth to another.

If you find yourself struggling to maintain an altitude of consciousness during a reading, you can get help from the person's Masters, Teachers, and Loved Ones by asking, "Where is the Light here? Please show me. Keep me connected to the Light so I can help elevate this Soul to its next-best version of itself—to its next-highest level of goodness." Then, be still while the Masters, Teachers, and Loved Ones show you what you need to see.

Of course, maintaining an altitude of consciousness does not just apply when you're reading for others. It's equally important to maintain this perspective when you're reading for yourself. Do you hear criticism, sarcasm, or judgment when you open your Akashic Records? Does the information sound less like your Masters, Teachers, and Loved Ones and more like your own self-talk? Then, ask to be shown the Truth about yourself and the answers you are seeking. Again, if you're feeling resistance or if those negative thoughts persist, know that there is nothing to fear. You're surrounded by Light and love, and you've been imbued with the courage to know the Truth—which is always, ultimately, helpful and positive.

Here is a meditation you can use to help you strengthen your altitude of consciousness. Open your Akashic Records before beginning the meditation. Then, read the following words slowly, pausing between paragraphs to close your eyes and visualize each scene or idea.

MEDITATION

Open your awareness to your relationship with your own Akashic Records.

Open yourself up to the presence of your own Masters, Teachers, and Loved Ones. To the best of your ability, be open to the reality of their wisdom and compassion for you. This is a group whose commitment to you is so deep and so unshakable that there's nothing you can do to scare them or push them away. They're always there for you.

Find out from your Masters, Teachers, and Loved Ones how they see you as an agent for the Akashic Records—how they perceive your relationship with the Records and how working in the Records supports you.

You have been called into the Akasha at this point because of who you are. Ask your Masters, Teachers, and Loved Ones: "Why now? Why this personality? Why this incarnation?" What do they say about the role of the Akashic Records in the transformation of the planet at this time? How do they see your participation, through the Records, in the transformation and healing of the life force on the planet at this time?

Allow yourself to become aware of the pillar of Light that is raining down all around you. Take your individual pillar of Light and allow it to merge with the pillar of Light that's been established by all students of the Akasha. It is here . . . now . . . anchored, and it goes as far as your consciousness will take you . . . and then it goes out from there.

Step into the pillar of Light and face out. As you look out, you can see points of Light spreading out across the globe, Souls awakening to the Light in themselves and in others. See the Light spreading out, one Soul at a time.

There's an expansion, an amplification, a quickening of Light—so much so that the entire continent is full of points of Light . . . connecting with other points of Light . . . and spreading across the world . . . until the most obvious and dominant force on the planet is the Light of the eternal Soul.

Let it be.

Now, bring your attention back to this moment and this book, and close your Akashic Records.

FROM INITIATE TO BEGINNING PRACTITIONER

Congratulations! Having gotten this far in the book, you now know how to use the Pathway Prayer Process to Access the Heart of the Akashic Records. Now that you have this knowledge, you can use the information in part 2 to strengthen your own work in the Records while you learn to work with others as an Akashic Records Practitioner.

PART TWO

USING THE AKASHIC RECORDS TO HEAL YOURSELF AND OTHERS

5

Energy Healing in the Akashic Records

Welcome to your next level of work in the Akashic Records. This level involves deepening your understanding of how the Records help people achieve healing. As we begin to explore energy healing in the Records, it may be useful to review the meaning of the word "heal": "to cause an undesirable condition to be overcome; to restore to original purity or integrity; to return to a sound state." These forms of healing occur naturally in the Records because every Akashic Record reading allows us to see ourselves as we are seen, known, and loved by our Masters, Teachers, and Loved Ones: essentially pure and sound. When we see our purity and soundness during a reading and begin to know this Truth about ourselves, our knowing then becomes the first step in our healing. This helps us begin to restore ourselves to our original purity and integrity, to our original sound state—and in this way our healing begins.

At this point you may be asking yourself, *If seeing myself differently is all it takes to start healing, then why can't I do it myself? Why do I need the Akashic Records to tell me who I am? I already know who I am.* The answer is both simple and complex. When we humans look at our lives, our perceptions are limited both *by* and *to* our current physical bodies having our current earthly experiences in this current human lifetime. So, from our human perspective, we see illness and imperfection. We often feel that something's wrong or missing, that we are not "the whole enchilada." Yet when we have a chance to view our true essence from the perspective of the Records, we see a different picture. By our very nature as manifestations of the Divine Source, our true essence is eternal wholeness, eternal wellness, and eternal goodness. Not only are we the whole enchilada, we're "all that and a bag of chips"! At the Soul level, this is always the case. As is often said, we are Divine Beings in physical bodies having human experiences on this planet. The Akashic Records shed Light on this Truth, and they help us remember and internalize it so we don't have to stay caught up in illusion.

One of the great paradoxes of the spiritual journey is that, at the Soul level, we are perfect in every way, yet in our current physical form, we may be suffering some very real limitations, such as mental or physical illness, chronic disease, financial hardship, or relationship problems. As we walk our spiritual paths, we are asked to hold within ourselves these seemingly conflicting Truths. So while our infinite Soul is perfect and flawless, our finite human self may be suffering from a terminal illness. One way to reconcile this paradox is to recognize that these two Truths exist simultaneously in two different dimensions. The Soul-level Truth of perfection exists in the invisible dimension within, while the physical Truth of illness exists in the visible, external dimension. Yet these two Truths do not negate each other; they merely coexist until we leave our physical body and become entirely spirit and entirely whole at the end of this current lifetime.

Understanding this spiritual paradox allows us to recognize that illnesses and disasters of any kind are neither indictments nor expressions of the condition of the Soul. Rather, they are experiences that we encounter as humans for the purpose of learning to love ourselves and others in spite of—or, oftentimes, *because* of—those illnesses or disasters.

HOW DOES ENERGY HEALING OCCUR IN THE AKASHIC RECORDS?

How do you help your clients remember their essential wholeness? Well, unlike other energy healers, as an Akashic reader-practitioner you do not send, direct, remove, or manipulate a client's energy during a reading. Instead, you open the client's Records and ask the Light of the Akasha to reveal that Soul's true essence so, for the duration of the reading (and to a certain extent, afterward), that person can experience themself from the altitude of consciousness that the Records provide. As the reader, you merely "flip the switch" that allows this en-Lightenment to begin. Then, as you speak the Truth during the reading, the Light of the Records intensifies and accelerates, and the information is transmitted to your client on the energy of your spoken words. When the energy and information are sufficiently registered in your client's consciousness and physical being, they cause a shift, an expansion, and an opening, which enable healing to occur at whatever levels are necessary—mental, physical, emotional, spiritual, energetic, Soul, or any combination thereof.

Though your client may not immediately recognize that any kind of healing has occurred, you as the reader understand that most healings in the Records begin with subtle openings in people's awareness. Those openings then lead to deeper shifts that empower people to begin releasing unhealthy thoughts and habits and replacing them with ones that significantly enrich their lives. And in every case, what allows for these healings is the realization of the Truth: that we are never separate from our Source of Creation. Therefore, we are always—in every moment and despite all earthly appearances—good, whole, well, and sound. As we make our way back to realizing this Soul-level Truth, we are in a state of grace that allows ongoing healing to occur—if only, at first, on the subtlest of levels.

AS AN AKASHIC RECORDS PRACTITIONER, WHAT ARE MY ROLES AND RESPONSIBILITIES?

One way of looking at your role as an Akashic Records Practitioner is to imagine yourself as a restorer of artifacts and your clients as crystal-clear vessels that have gathered dust through the ages. Some of the vessels are covered with so much dust that it's difficult to see their hidden beauty. When viewed superficially, they may even appear unattractive or flawed. Yet, once they're cleaned with a sonic device, the dust shakes loose, and you can see their perfection. However, you must perform this process delicately. Increasing the sonic vibration too quickly or too much can damage some vessels, but increasing the vibration at just the right pace will gently loosen the dust and restore them to their original integrity.

As a practitioner of the Akashic Records, your role is to allow the transmission of Akashic *energy* first and *information* second. This order is necessary because the energetic vibration of the Records is what the information travels on. So by "bathing" your clients in this energy and giving them information, you allow them to "shed their dust" so they can see their true selves in the Light of the Records.

Though your role may appear simple on the surface, the preparation involved in becoming a good reader is of vital importance and may take some time and effort. Your personal preparation is an ongoing inner process that involves understanding yourself at the level of Soul and realizing your own Soul-level wholeness and wellness.

As you work in your own Records and in the Records of others, a natural healing occurs. By consciously, responsibly, and deliberately placing yourself in the energy of the Records, you begin this healing process. Each time you open the Records, peace, love, light, and goodness surround and infuse you, filling you and your energy field with the higher quality of the Akashic life force. As this happens, there is a quickening of the energetic vibrations both inside and around you, and any vibrations that are ready to move at a more rapid rate will do so. You then experience those accelerated vibrations as elevated feelings and heightened senses.

Whenever you access the Akashic Records, the energy of the Akasha meets your human energy and causes a kind of "ignition," as the Light of the Akasha (which is extremely fast and refined yet indestructible) meets your slower, heavier human energy. When this happens, the lighter energies join together to create a faster vibration, and the heavier, denser energies—associated with negative emotions and repetitive thought patterns—fall away and are absorbed by the earth's energy field. There, they are transmuted into energy patterns that are more useful on the physical plane. So, merely by being in the Records, you receive an "energetic tune-up" that helps you refine and elevate your own energy and serve your clients more effectively.

As I mentioned when explaining the Pathway Prayer, the interface of Akashic and human energy begins about eighteen inches above your crown, at your eighth chakra. At that point, the Akashic energy flows through a hollow tube (or pillar) of Light, through which the Akashic energy moves into your infinite, interior dimension. This dimension connects you to the Universe through the person you are in this lifetime. In this dimension, you can find your current emotional makeup, the structure and patterns of your mind, the resources of your will, your dreams, your Soul, your relationship with the Divine, and all other parts of yourself that you know to be true but cannot see with your physical eyes.

Whether your heavier, denser energies accelerate or fall away, they are always used for good in other situations. No energy, whether identified as "positive" or "negative," is ever lost or wasted. Every atomic point of Light is useful in its right place, and the Light of the Akasha facilitates the distribution of energy to its right place in the Universe. For us humans, this experience usually registers as emotional or mental shifts. During emotional shifts, the denser, slower energies expressed as sadness, fear, despair, resentment, anger, and frustration are transmuted to higher, quicker energies expressed as happiness, contentment, freedom, and joy. By being present in the Records—even if you're reading for someone else—you can experience such a shift. So if you were sad or uncertain about something before you opened the Records, you may find that after the reading, you suddenly have clarity and hope. And if you were confused about an impending decision, you might suddenly know what to do.

So far, I've been addressing your practitioner preparation as it occurs through the Akashic Records. There's another kind of preparation, however, that involves your active and deliberate participation. Doing effective work in the Records and becoming the best reader you can be requires taking responsibility for who you are, where you are in life, and how you are dealing with the life you are living. The more you take responsibility to resolve your personal issues and clear them from your mind and body, the more space you make within yourself to accommodate more Light and health.

Just to be clear, taking responsibility for yourself should not be confused with taking the blame for others' beliefs and actions.

You are only responsible for yourself and for doing the best you can. So, in this context, taking responsibility means accepting your life without blaming, and understanding that everything has a divine purpose, even if it's not always obvious. Acceptance in this way is neither a sign of resignation nor defeat. Hardly. Instead, it means arriving at a place of peace and being able to say to yourself, *This is who I am, and this is my life. I'll change whatever I can, and I'll release what I cannot change. Either way, I'm doing my best. And by doing my best as an individual, I'm contributing to the highest good of all. I no longer need to look to any other person to make things better for me. I accept responsibility for my life, and I'll make choices for myself. And I'll enjoy the results of those choices while I am here on this earth.*

Getting to a place of peace and personal responsibility will require you to look within to find those patterns of thinking, feeling, and behaving that have been causing you pain. Fortunately, you have the Akashic Records to help you with this process. With the guidance of your Masters, Teachers, and Loved Ones, you can safely examine who you are and be honest about the areas that need work. You can then begin to make changes in your life that support your new spiritual direction, open you up to accommodate more Light, and allow you to live from a place of compassion and grace.

As you will discover while working in your Records, the way to experience the greatest relief, freedom, joy, and peace is to remove your attention from others and what they have not done and instead examine yourself. As you ask yourself, *How have I responded? What is my part in this situation? Why am I stopping myself from being kind and loving?*, you will begin to discover ways to heal yourself.

The process of self-discovery and healing is ongoing. It's like a school that meets all year round, and as this life-school goes on, things ebb and flow. There will be times when you feel peaceful and happy and free. Other times, you will become stuck in old ideas and behaviors and feel like you're barely making progress. Such times are inevitable for all human beings. Just find a quiet place and open your Records. Your Masters, Teachers, and Loved Ones will be happy to lend support and help you restore harmony and balance.

At times, this work can seem overwhelming, yet it's a necessary part of being a responsible Akashic Records Practitioner. As you continue on this path of personal responsibility, you will grow in understanding and love for yourself and others. These qualities will shine through you, making you a beacon of Light and healing for everyone you encounter. Your skill and success as an Akashic Records Practitioner will depend on your relationship with yourself, your own healing process, and your willingness to be led by the forces of Light. As you do these things, you will naturally realize your potential to radiate love and goodwill into your world and to assist others with understanding, kindness, and power through your Akashic Records readings.

As you move more deeply into energy healing in the Records, you'll discover that your level of personal preparation will determine your ability to get out of the way so healing can occur most effectively for your clients. You'll also discover that your knowledge and understanding of the *process itself* will facilitate your clients' healing. There are several reasons for this:

- Doing your own energy-healing work in the Records gives you firsthand knowledge of how the process works. As you become more familiar with the three levels of energy healing (which we will discuss shortly), you will recognize more quickly the energetic shift that occurs at each level. Then, your ability to recognize these shifts during your own readings will help you recognize them in your clients' readings. Consequently, you'll be able to help your clients more easily accommodate the accelerated energy of the Light and more deeply anchor its healing vibration.

- Doing your own energy-healing work in the Records helps you learn to trust the process, which helps you get out of your own way. Remember the part of the Opening Prayer that says, "Protect me from all forms of self-centeredness, and direct my attention to the work at hand"? If you have faith in the process and your ability to apply it, you'll be able to hold steady in the Light and keep focused on your client without being distracted by unnecessary worries or fears.
- Speaking of getting out of your own way: Doing your own energy-healing work in the Records is the quickest way to develop a clear altitude of consciousness. A well-developed altitude of consciousness helps you free yourself of your own "dust," which frees you of judgments, attitudes, and reactions—both in and out of the Records.
- Allowing your personal feelings to surface during a reading obstructs the flow of Light and blocks your ability to recognize the Soul-level Truth about a person or situation. However, when you've cleared your own judgments and know the Truth about yourself, it is much easier to recognize the Truth about another. So rather than judge a person from your human perspective and consciousness, you are able to say to yourself, *Because I know this Soul's divine nature as I know my own, I know that this person's goodness and wholeness are there. I will follow the Light until I see this Soul's true essence and can help them see it too.* In a way, this process is like digging for gold: When you're

certain it's there, you keep digging because you know the deeper you go, the closer you are to striking it rich. But if you're working with "faulty equipment," the process becomes a lot more difficult—if not impossible at times.

Let's sum things up thus far. Your role as an Akashic Records Practitioner is to use the energy and information of the Records to recognize the Soul-level Truth of your own essence, as well as each client's essence. Then, as you give a reading, that Soul-level recognition will elevate and shift your client's energy and perspective so they can recognize the Truth too and healing can occur. That is both your role and your goal. Unfortunately, though, it may not be the conscious goal of the client for whom you are reading!

Though at some basic level, all Souls desire to experience their wholeness and Oneness with all of Creation, not all *humans* who come to you for a reading are consciously aware of this desire. In other words, they aren't "feeling the love" right then—for themselves or for others. So if you're doing a reading for "Joe," for example, and you begin telling him how lovely he is (because that is his true essence as revealed by his Masters, Teachers, and Loved Ones), he may find what you're saying so disconcerting that his first instinct will be to reject it and insist that it's not true. Especially if he has come for guidance about a "mistake" he perceives he has made, his thoughts about himself in that moment will be anything but positive and kind. So the Akashic information you're sharing with Joe will not match what he "knows" about himself, and energetically, he will be unable to receive it.

What do you do in this situation? First of all, remain unflappable. It's okay. Joe's okay. You're okay. Recognize the Truth behind Joe's reaction, and don't let it throw you out of the Light and into your own thoughts, fears, and judgments. Instead, hold steady for a moment. Take a deep breath, take a sip of water, and/or say the silent part of the Prayer to yourself again: *Help me to know Joseph Alan Woodside in the Light of the Akashic Records, to see Joseph Alan Woodside through the eyes of the Lords of the Records, and enable me to share the wisdom and compassion that the Masters, Teachers, and Loved Ones of Joseph Alan Woodside have for him.* Or you can shorten that prayer to "Help!" and trust that Joe's Masters, Teachers, and Loved Ones will keep you centered in the Light so you can receive their guidance.

In such a moment, it's extremely important to understand that this may be the first time in quite a while that Joe has heard good things about himself, and the mismatch in perceptions may be so jarring that he is neither willing nor able to accept what is true. On one level, for example, he may feel that you're messing with his "comfortable" and familiar picture of himself; it's as if he's looking in a mirror and expecting to see what he always sees, but the image you're reflecting back to him is so alien, he finds it downright scary. On another level, Joe may sense that you—equipped with the laser-like Light of the Akasha—are poking holes in the illusory facade he's constructed in order to rationalize his unwillingness to understand, forgive, change, decide, heal, and move forward in his life. . . . But he is here for a reading, isn't he? Despite all of human Joe's kicking and screaming, the eternal Soul currently known as Joseph Alan Woodside has shown up for his healing. This brave Soul is calling for help because he cannot do it alone, and you are answering the call. And it is precisely in moments such as this when all of your personal healing work in the Records will support you as a reader-practitioner. It is also when you must begin to follow what I call the Three Levels of Healing in the Akashic Records.

THE THREE LEVELS OF HEALING IN THE AKASHIC RECORDS

The permanent resolution of any problem requires a permanent evolution of the Soul. In other words, in order for people to have any kind of healing in the Records, they must first experience a permanent shift in the way they perceive themselves. Then, that new perception can eventually lead to a shift in the way they treat themselves. But sometimes, as in Joe's case, people can't experience those shifts unless you, the Akashic reader-practitioner, lead them through the Three Levels of Healing: Understand the story from the client's point of view, look for the causes and conditions, and recognize the Soul-level Truth.

Level 1: Understand the Story from the Client's Point of View

During this first level of healing, you will work at the level of the problem and its physical manifestations. When people come to you for readings, it's usually because they have a problem or situation they can't resolve on their own. They may be upset, angry, hurt, confused, or even desperate, and you may be their last resort. So the first thing to do after you've opened a client's Records is to listen to their story. Allow your client to describe the problem as they currently see it—what it is, how and when it started, who else is involved, and what complications it has caused. While you listen, completely accept the person and the story without judgment or preconceived notions because you know that this human being has been doing the best they can. You also know that what you are hearing is this person's transitory Truth, as told from their human perspective, and that it is not necessarily the Soul-level Truth.

Since energy travels on the spoken word, your client's verbal acknowledgment of the problem is the first step in the healing process. Here's an example of how it works. Let's say "Jillian" comes to you for a reading. After obtaining her current legal name, you say the Opening Prayer to access Jillian's Akashic Records. Once her Records are open, you say, "I can see that you're upset. Can you tell me what's going on?" Jillian then explains that she's distraught and overwhelmed because she's in the middle of a lengthy divorce. She's angry and bitter, and she can't stand it anymore. She goes on to describe the details of the divorce, including how and why the proceedings began and how the divorce is affecting her life.

While Jillian speaks, your job is to hear her story and understand it from her point of view. Rather than sit in judgment of Jillian, her husband, or the process of divorce itself, stay with her and her story. Don't project your own experiences or compare her to anyone you know. Just sit and listen, and be the wide-open conduit who allows information to be received and transmitted for the duration of the reading.

It may seem like nothing significant happens during this level of Jillian's reading. Yet, if she can tell you her story, and you can hear it without judgment, the first level of healing will occur. Here's what happens: When you open Jillian's Records, you "ring the Akashic doorbell" and ask the Akasha to enter your consciousness and surround you and Jillian in Light. You then initiate the healing by asking Jillian to tell her story. As she begins to speak, the energy of her words allows the Light of the Akasha to intensify and accelerate its vibration. The more you listen to Jillian with compassion and understanding, the quicker you allow the Light to do its work, and the quicker you both allow yourselves to resonate to the Light's accelerated vibration. Once that acceleration occurs, you and Jillian receive the energetic "jump-start" you need to move to level two.

Level 2: Look for the Causes and Conditions

This level of healing moves you into the domain of causes and conditions. After a client has finished describing their problem, you can ask the Records to reveal its causes and conditions. Sometimes a cause can be physical, as in the case of someone who was born with a certain disease or who developed cancer after working with asbestos for many years. At other times, a cause can be mental or emotional, as in the case of someone having a particular belief or attitude that causes something to happen—or that precludes it from happening. At other times, a cause can be "invisible" and due to certain past-life experiences, choices, beliefs, or ancestral influences.

Some problems can be healed at level two when information about the cause or condition is all that's required. Put another way, when a lack of understanding is the problem, information is the solution. For example, while telling his story during level one of a reading, "Larry" describes his problem as chronic laryngitis, for which his doctors have been unable to determine either a cause or cure. So you ask Larry's Masters, Teachers, and Loved Ones to reveal the origin of his problem. They show you a past life in which the Soul now known as Larry was hanged for publicly voicing his beliefs, and you relate the details of this experience to Larry just as you receive them. When you finish, Larry says, "Oh, man! I get it now! This laryngitis thing started a few years ago after a protest rally I organized. At first, I blamed myself for the problem: I thought I had shouted too much that day and damaged my vocal chords. But when the doctors examined me, that turned out not to be true. What I now understand *is* true is that my latent fear of being hanged for speaking out made me lose my voice that day—both literally and figuratively—since it was the last rally I ever organized or attended."

For Larry, this moment of Truth is all that he needs for healing. He knows that, while there are possible consequences to voicing his beliefs in public in this lifetime, it is unlikely he will be hanged. This Akashic information, as transmitted through the energy of *your* voice, moves Larry into the awareness that there's no problem with him or *his* voice. He lets go of his fear and gains a sense of peace. And, in time, he regains not only his physical voice but his courage to speak out at future rallies.

Although the information revealed during level two can be extremely helpful—and perhaps, as in Larry's case, maybe all a person needs to solve a problem—it is still considered transitory Truth because you are viewing a particular Soul in the context of a past human incarnation rather than as its true essence as a divine, eternal being.

When the information revealed at this level is not enough to dispel the problem, or even loosen its grip, it's time to move to level three.

Level 3: Recognize the Soul-Level Truth

Whereas level one is about your clients being heard, level three is about them being *known*. Level three is the domain of essential, permanent, Soul-level Truth. It's the level at which you as the reader are able to see a person as they are seen, known, and loved in the Akashic Records. Working in this level allows you to transcend the realm of the person's mundane, earthly problem and move into the realm of divine consciousness. It is from this level that you can see that whatever a client is experiencing right now—drug addiction, illness, divorce, the aftermath of an accident—it is actually perfect and necessary because it's the most effective vehicle for allowing this client's Soul growth.

Let's go back to Joe again. If you were talking to him at this level, you might find yourself telling him what a strong and brave Soul his Masters, Teachers, and Loved Ones know he is for choosing such a difficult lesson or path. Even if he's still balking at hearing about his goodness because he's still having trouble seeing the Truth, *you* will have no trouble seeing Joe for the awesome Soul he is. You also will have no trouble understanding that although Joe may think his "vessel" is tarnished or flawed, he always holds within him the potential and the means for change. So if Joe can't "shake his dust loose" right now, don't push him. For some reason, he feels the need to hold on to it. Rushing or forcing Joe's process right now could actually cause him harm. So rather than judging him for feeling this way, keep telling him the Truth that his Records are revealing.

For example, you might tell him that even if *he* doesn't know it right now, his Masters, Teachers, and Loved Ones know that he is much more than his physical body and circumstances, that his Soul can never be sick, and that even though he may feel quite distant from God right now, he is always connected to God and all of God's creation. Energetically speaking, what we focus on expands, so by allowing Joe to focus on these Truths, you are providing him the opportunity to open his heart and expand his view of himself.

As you speak with Joe, keep remembering that the energy of the Akashic Records is being transmitted through the sound of your voice. You don't need to direct the energy; the Light will go where it needs to go and will provide what it needs to provide. As long as you relate the Truth about Joe, he will resonate to its vibration and begin to receive his healing—even if that healing involves making peace with his transitory human illness or imperfection, and even if it means understanding that sometimes it's the illness or imperfection itself that leads to the deepest Soul healing and the richest experience of coming to know God.

As you move out of level three and prepare to close the Records, it's important to remember that the outcome of a reading is never up to you. Your responsibility begins and ends with you being as spiritually fit as possible to maintain the integrity of the Records and assist each Soul on its journey. Whatever your clients do with what you give them is entirely up to them. Some clients may walk away from their readings and promptly forget about them. Others may assimilate the information over time and apply it as they are able. Still others may jump up at the end of their reading and decide to change their lives in that moment. Again, whatever they decide, it is not in your control. Letting go of the belief that it *is* will "protect you from all forms of self-centeredness." Hold on to the belief, instead, that on some level, every person will "get it" at exactly the right time—if not in this lifetime, then in the next . . . or the next . . . or the next.

HOW CAN I RECOGNIZE THE THREE LEVELS OF HEALING?

The exercises that follow will help you familiarize yourself with the Three Levels of Healing in the Records. The first exercise will help you practice working in your own Akashic Records. The second exercise will help you practice working with someone else.

Note: Though I've broken each exercise into three separate readings to facilitate your learning, all three levels may also occur within a single reading.

EXERCISE

The Three Levels of Healing
Working with Your Own Akashic Records

LEVEL 1: TELL YOUR STORY FROM YOUR POINT OF VIEW

1. Think of a problem or situation that's "alive" for you right now and with which you would like some help.

2. Use the Opening Prayer to access your Akashic Records.

3. Tell your Masters, Teachers, and Loved Ones your story. (Write it down or say it out loud, whichever is easier for you.) As you describe the problem from your perspective, include such details as how and when it started, who is involved, what impact it has had so far, and what complications it has caused.

4. While you are describing your problem, pause every so often and ask yourself these questions:
   - How do I feel about myself right now? Am I judging myself in any way? (e.g., I'm good/I'm bad; I'm right/I'm wrong; I shouldn't have thought, said, or done that.)
   - How do I feel about the problem or situation? Am I judging it in any way? (e.g., It's stupid; It's crazy; It's wrong; It makes me miserable every day; It never should have happened; I was totally justified in my actions; Everyone else is wrong!)

5. If you find yourself being judgmental in any way, ask your Masters, Teachers, and Loved Ones to help you understand that, in this particular moment, you don't have a complete picture of the problem, nor are you seeing yourself or others for who they truly are. Also ask your Masters, Teachers, and Loved Ones to help you see that your situation is neither good nor bad; it just is. Likewise, your feelings about yourself and the situation are neither good nor bad; they just are. Of course, they are! And whatever they are, they're okay at this time, so finish telling your story without judgment.

6. When you've finished telling your story, you're likely to sense a shift. It may feel like a sigh of relief, as if relating your problem without judgment has helped you get it off your chest—literally clear its heavy energy from your heart space—and you're starting to breathe a bit easier. You may also begin to see yourself and your problem from a broader, more compassionate perspective.

7. In this state of expanded awareness, say the Closing Prayer to exit your Akashic Records.

LEVEL 2: ASK ABOUT THE CAUSES AND CONDITIONS

1. Recall the problem or situation you described during your level-one reading. (If you wrote about your problem, you may want to review your notes.) Then, use the Prayer to open your Akashic Records.

2. Ask your Masters, Teachers, and Loved Ones to show you the cause of your problem. If you need any help getting started, here are some questions you might use:
   - Did the problem begin in this lifetime? If so, what was its cause? (e.g., Was it hereditary or environmental? Was it something I did or said? Was it an opinion or a belief that I held or still hold? Was it something that I am not seeing?)
   - What lesson can I learn from this particular problem, and how is it assisting my Soul's growth?
   - What information can you give me that will help me shift my current perspective and move toward resolution and healing?

- Please help me identify ways in which the choices I made were beneficial for me. How is it possible that this horrible mess is somehow my best effort to expand my experience of love in this lifetime?

Or:

- Did my problem begin in another lifetime? If so, can you show me the causes and conditions?
- How and why did I carry the problem into this current lifetime?
- If I still need to work on the problem in this lifetime, what do I need to know or do so I can begin to resolve it?
- Please help me identify ways in which the choices I made then were beneficial for me. How is it possible that the mess is somehow my best effort to expand my experience of love then and now?

3. As your Masters, Teachers, and Loved Ones reveal the cause of your problem, you may find that you have an Aha moment that helps you shift your perspective dramatically and begin to move toward healing. When you feel that you've sufficiently registered this shift, close your Akashic Records by saying the Closing Prayer.

Or:

4. If you're having any trouble understanding or accepting what your Masters, Teachers, and Loved Ones are saying, don't struggle. Close your Akashic Records and sit with the information for a while. You will have

another chance to gain clarity when you open your Records for level three.

LEVEL 3: RECOGNIZE THE SOUL-LEVEL TRUTH

1. Use the Prayer to open your Akashic Records.

2. Recall your level-two reading. If its energy and information were sufficient to shift your perspective and anchor your healing, ask your Masters, Teachers, and Loved Ones to show you how you are seen, known, and loved in the Records. In other words, ask them to show you your Soul's true essence in a way that helps you see it too. Also ask them to show you how this particular problem was perfect for your Soul's growth.

3. Spend some more time in your Records and allow yourself to be bathed in the Light of the Akasha. Let it strengthen and raise your vibration and help you realize who you are. Then, when you feel ready, say the Closing Prayer and exit your Records.

Or:

4. If you're still having trouble understanding or accepting what your Masters, Teachers, and Loved Ones said during your level-two reading, ask them to help you see the Soul-level Truth of who you are. If that Truth is too difficult to accept right now, ask them to help you accept the fact that where you are at this moment is where you need to be. It is the perfect context in which to learn this particular Soul lesson; and eventually, in your own time, you will find peace and resolution.

5. When you feel ready, say the Closing Prayer and exit your Akashic Records.

EXERCISE

The Three Levels of Healing
Working in Someone Else's Akashic Records

LEVEL 1: UNDERSTAND THE STORY FROM THE CLIENT'S POINT OF VIEW

1. Ask someone who is open to Akashic Record readings to help you with this exercise. Tell the person that you will be doing this exercise for practice and will be going into their Records three times. Ask the person to prepare for this first reading by thinking of a problem or situation they are struggling with right now.

2. Before you open the person's Records, tell them to ask this question periodically throughout the reading: Am I being judged in any way right now? If the answer is ever yes, the person should tell you when it is happening.

3. Use the Opening Prayer and the person's current legal name to access their Akashic Records.

4. Ask the person to share their story with you and their Masters, Teachers, and Loved Ones. As the person describes the problem or situation, listen for details, like how and when it started, who is involved, what impact it has had so far, and what complications it has caused.

5. Also, while you listen, ask yourself these questions:
   - How do I feel about this person right now? Am I judging them in any way? (e.g., Wow, what a mean/stupid/irritating person! No wonder people avoid them; What are they thinking? I'm not liking them very much right now; Wow, what a sweet/thoughtful/kindhearted person! I wish I could be more like them; How brave and strong they are to have to deal with such a lout of a boss. They don't deserve such treatment; Oh, my gosh! They are just like my boss/coworker/boyfriend/brother. I know their type exactly!)
   - How do I feel about the problem or situation? Am I judging it in any way? (e.g., It's stupid; It's crazy; It's wrong; It never should have happened, but I can certainly see why it did; Jim's argument with his brother sounds a lot like the fight I had with my sister. I already know what Jim should do if he wants to solve this problem.)

6. If you find yourself being judgmental in any way, ask the person's Masters, Teachers, and Loved Ones to help you understand that, in this particular moment, you don't have a complete picture of what's happening, nor are you seeing the person for who they truly are. Also ask the Masters, Teachers, and Loved Ones to help you see that this person and the problem are neither good nor bad; they just are. Then, from this new perspective, continue listening without judgment.

7. Is it possible that this situation is somehow for the benefit of your client? Is it possible that they made

decisions to expand their personal experience of being known and loved? How is that possible?

8. When the person has finished telling their story, one or both of you are likely to sense a shift. To you, it might feel as if your heart has opened and allowed you to see this person from a different, nonjudgmental perspective. To the other person, it might feel as if relating the problem without being judged has cleared it from their heart space and shifted their perspective as well.

9. In this new state of expansion and awareness, say the Closing Prayer to exit the person's Akashic Records.

LEVEL 2: LOOK FOR THE CAUSES AND CONDITIONS

1. Use the Opening Prayer to enter the person's Akashic Records.

2. Ask the Masters, Teachers, and Loved Ones to reveal the cause of the problem the person described in level one. If you need any help getting started, here are some questions you can use:
   - Did the problem begin in this lifetime? If so, what was its cause? (e.g., Was it hereditary or environmental? Was it something this person did or said? Was it an opinion or a belief that this person held or is still holding? Was it something that this person is not seeing?)

- What lesson can the person learn from this particular problem, and how is it assisting their Soul's growth?
- What other information can you give me to help this person shift their current perspective and move toward resolution and healing?
- In what ways did my client make choices to intentionally expand their sense of being safe and loved?

Or:

- Did the problem begin in another lifetime? If so, what are its causes and conditions?
- How and why did this person carry the problem into this current lifetime?
- In what ways did my client choose to allow this difficulty to expand their sense of being safe and loved then and even now?
- If the problem has served its purpose and usefulness, how can this person let it go?
- If the person still needs to work on the problem in this lifetime, what do they need to know in order to begin to resolve it?

3. As the person's Masters, Teachers, and Loved Ones reveal the cause of the problem, they may have an Aha moment that shifts their perspective dramatically and initiates healing. When you feel that the person has sufficiently registered this shift, you can close their Akashic Records.

4. If the person is having trouble understanding or accepting what the Masters, Teachers, and Loved Ones are saying, don't struggle. Close the Records and let the person sit with this new information for a while. You will have another chance to gain clarity when you open their Records for level three.

LEVEL 3: RECOGNIZE THE SOUL-LEVEL TRUTH

1. Use the Prayer to open the person's Akashic Records.

2. If the information you received during level two was enough to provide clarity and healing, you can move on to the next step. Ask the Masters, Teachers, and Loved Ones to show you how this person is seen, known, and loved in the Records. Find out how to communicate this awareness to your client. In other words, ask the Masters, Teachers, and Loved Ones to show you this Soul's true essence in a way that helps your client see it too.

3. Spend some time in the person's Akashic Records and allow them to be immersed in their energy and information. Let the Light of the Akasha strengthen and raise their vibration (and yours) as you help them realize the Soul-level Truth.

4. When the time is right, say the Closing Prayer to exit the person's Akashic Records.

Or:

5. If the person is still having trouble understanding or accepting what the Masters, Teachers, and Loved Ones said during level two, ask them to help you show this person the Soul-level Truth of their essence. Make sure you are open to recognizing the perfection and magnificence of your client. Ask the Masters, Teachers, and Loved Ones to help you and the person accept and appreciate who they are right at that moment, no matter where they are in the healing process.

6. When the time is right, say the Prayer and close the Akashic Records.

6

Healing Ancestral Patterns in the Akashic Records

As you do more and more Akashic readings for yourself and others, you may begin to notice something interesting: The causes of people's problems in this lifetime are very often due to beliefs, attitudes, or behavioral patterns they've inherited from their ancestors. So exploring your ancestral lineage and freeing yourself from detrimental ancestral patterns are the next logical steps for healing work in the Records.

Doing ancestral work in the Records is also natural and logical because all past and present occurrences, as well as all future probabilities, are held within the Akasha. So you can work in the Records to learn not only how you're currently being affected by your ancestors, but also how you can make choices now that will affect future generations. In essence, working in the Akashic Records to heal your limiting ancestral patterns will help you:

- Explore the true nature of your ancestral lines
- Release inherited patterns of consciousness that are detrimental to your Soul's growth as well as the growth of your entire Soul-group
- Align with the highest probabilities of your ancestral lineage in order to assist in its future evolution

WHO ARE MY ANCESTORS?

People typically define their ancestors as their "family tree": past generations of relatives from whom they are directly descended. Although this definition is true in the Akashic Records, it is also true that, in the Records, your ancestors can be Souls you are related to in consciousness but not necessarily by birth. Further, given the Soul-level Truth that we are all One and are related by our shared DNA, when it comes right down to it, everyone is your ancestor! For the purposes of this work, we will use the Akashic description of "ancestors": anyone who is related to you on the Soul level, biologically or not.

As you experience lifetime after lifetime, you often travel in various ancestral Soul-groups that share the same personal, universal, and Soul-level goals. You will choose a particular group to simultaneously promote your own Soul's growth and the Soul growth of the group. As such, those in the group are committed to sticking together and helping each other experience situations that help you all realize your goals. Regardless of the group's lesser or intermediate goals, its ultimate goal is always the same: to achieve peace among all of its members. This goal is not usually accomplished quickly or even in one lifetime. Rather, it's accomplished over a series of lifetimes, during which you all grow incrementally, one generation at a time, as you learn to balance your "karmic opposites."

For example, let's say that two Souls within an ancestral group make an agreement to help each other learn a lesson in unconditional love. In one lifetime, the two Souls incarnate: one as a wealthy oligarch and the other as an unhoused person whom he passes on the street every day. For each of these Souls, their roles afford them countless opportunities to experience unconditional love: *How can I love myself now?* Then, in subsequent lifetimes, these same two Souls continue to shift their roles, and choose the contexts in which to enact them, so they can discover what it feels like to be on both sides of the karmic coin. Ultimately, when both Souls have experienced a wholly complete expression of unconditional love, they will be at peace with each other and will exist in harmony. At that point, each Soul will be free to join other ancestral groups in order to have other kinds of experiences and learn other kinds of lessons.

As for your ancestral group in this lifetime, many of its members are indeed biologically related. Others, however, are related by their desire to carry out a shared goal. Regardless of how your ancestral group is connected, you will stay together—for better or for worse—until your karmic work is complete and you have grown to love one another. *How* you interact with each other will vary; sometimes you'll be kind and compassionate, and at other times, you'll be vengeful and mean-spirited. It really doesn't matter as long as you're fulfilling your karmic roles within your ancestral lines—and you end up loving each other when all is said and done.

HOW DO SOULS JOIN ANCESTRAL LINES?

Your ancestral Soul-group in this lifetime consists of different "intersecting" ancestral lines—some of which you chose to be born into and some of which you will choose later on in your life. As such, there are several ways your Soul can join different ancestral lines. The way in which most Souls join their main ancestral line is to be born into its family tree. In such a case, a particular line's members are all linked through their genetic code.

Another way Souls join ancestral lines is by being adopted into them. When a group of Souls is joined in this way, distinct karmic experiences ensue for the adopted child, the biological parents, and the adoptive parents and family.

Another way Souls join ancestral lines is to marry into them. It's often said that when you marry a person, you take on that person's whole tribe. This is especially true from an Akashic point of view since no matter how you get along with that "tribe," your choice to be with them is deliberate and is for a specific Soul purpose. Even if you try to escape your spouse's line by legally divorcing them, your connection to this line will remain active until your work with your ex-spouse is complete. So, if you've been divorced for a while but still actively resent your ex-spouse, go back and do the first exercise in chapter 5. While you're doing the exercise, find out what you can do to heal your resentment. That healing is only for you. Do what you can do since the only way to be free of a person is to have a peaceful parting. If you don't have a peaceful parting but struggle instead against "the ties that bind," you'll only make those ties tighter and more uncomfortable. If you achieve neutrality and peace, however, you'll relax the binding ties and move into a more comfortable position.

As I mentioned earlier, another way Souls join ancestral lines is by right of shared consciousness. In this case, every Soul in a specific ancestral line has agreed to be part of that line in order to raise its collective consciousness. If the line's karmic task is particularly challenging, its resolution may take several lifetimes. When the line has completed its task, however, the karmic ties will loosen and become inactive, and healing will occur among the line. The Souls will then be free to move on and join other ancestral lines.

WHAT IS MY RESPONSIBILITY TO MY ANCESTORS?

The person you are in this lifetime is the convergence point of all your relations and ancestral lines throughout your Soul's existence. As you work on yourself in this lifetime and find compassion and peace within, you release your judgment of not only yourself but others in your ancestral lines. And the more you are able to do this, the more you are able to bring growth and healing to your entire ancestral Soul-group, both now and in the future.

The most effective way to learn about yourself and heal karmic rifts—both within yourself and between you and others—is to work in your Akashic Records to gain the perspective they provide. Once you are able to accept the Soul-level Truth that the Records offer, you can change old beliefs, patterns, and behaviors and heal them for good. So focus on yourself, not others, and seek guidance on how to see situations for their Soul-level purposes and ultimate karmic benefits. Also ask to be shown your roles and responsibilities within your ancestral lines.

As you work to make peace with yourself, you allow for deep healing and transformation to occur. Even if you're the only one who's aware of what's happening, the shifts in you will open up space that allows for shifts in others, and your entire line will ascend. As you learn to be more accepting of others, you will find it easier to share whatever you have to give. This, in turn, will lessen others' need to tug on you in order to get what they need. When appropriate give-and-take is underway, everyone involved enjoys a new level of harmony and peace.

Even if you are alienated from your family, you can create a more peaceful and accepting environment. In fact, this is the karmic imperative of the black sheep. So don't worry that you are viewed this way; you really *are* a bit different from the rest. You are part of a rare and unusual breed that stands out from the herd, and you're the one people can't help but watch. With all eyes upon you, you have the opportunity to let go of your resistance to accepting people who are different. Ironically, you as the black sheep may want love, understanding, and acceptance from others, but then find—from the perspective of the Records—that *you* are the one who must *give* those things first to those who love, understand, and accept you the least.

As you accept your ancestors for who and what they are and are not, all of you are liberated. This is how you support the healing of your ancestral line. Be bold in your love, acceptance, and appreciation of everyone in the family, especially those who are difficult for you. The Records will give you the clarity and energy to fulfill your role, which will further the evolution of your current ancestral line and all the Souls who will join it in the future.

HOW CAN I EXPLORE MY ANCESTORS AND THEIR INFLUENCE ON MY LIFE?

The following exercises will help you explore one of your current ancestral lines. The questions are worded so you can ask them in your own Records and easily adapt them for use with your clients. Feel free to repeat these exercises as often as you'd like to explore different ancestral lines within your larger Soul-group.

As you work through each exercise, you may find that your Masters, Teachers, and Loved Ones choose to answer the questions as they are written. Alternatively, they may decide to combine one or more questions or answer them in a different order. However they decide to deliver the information, by the end of each reading, you will have your answers.

EXERCISE

Identify the Divine Intent of Your Lineage

PART A

1. Use the Opening Prayer to access your Akashic Records. Then, ask your Masters, Teachers, and Loved Ones the following questions about one of your ancestral lines:
   - Who are my ancestors?
   - What are the distinguishing traits of this particular ancestral line?
   - What is the divine intention of this line? (e.g., What is its Soul-level purpose? What are its short-term goals? Long-term goals?)
   - How do you (my Masters, Teachers, and Loved Ones) see these ancestors as a group moving through time and space?

2. Use the Closing Prayer to exit your Akashic Records. If you haven't been taking notes all along, write down any information from your reading that you found especially enlightening and would like to recall in the future.

PART B

1. Use the Opening Prayer to access your Records again. Then, ask the following questions:
   - What are the privileges and responsibilities of this particular ancestral line?
   - What are my individual privileges and responsibilities to this line?

- Which ancestral responsibilities have I taken on appropriately with this line, and why?
- How can I release the ancestral responsibilities that do not (and should not) belong to me?

2. Use the Closing Prayer to exit your Records. If you haven't already done so, write down any information from your reading that you would like to recall in the future.

EXERCISE

Explore the Space Between Lifetimes

PART A

1. Use the Opening Prayer to access your Records.

2. Ask your Masters, Teachers, and Loved Ones to take you on a "virtual tour" of the space between your lifetimes. This realm is sometimes called the Zone of Choice, or the Dimension of Choice, because in this dimension, your Soul makes choices for its next incarnation. Explore this dimension for a while. How does it look and feel to you? What is happening? Who or what is there?

3. Once you have a reasonable sense of where you are—and knowing that you can always come back to this place and explore it further in future readings—ask your Masters, Teachers, and Loved Ones to help you survey the family (the main ancestral line) you are in

right now. Then, ask these questions of your Masters, Teachers, and Loved Ones:
- Why have I chosen this particular ancestral line above all others?
- What can I learn or gain from them?
- What was I intending when I chose this group?
- Have I been with this group before?
- How is this group helping me realize the purposes of my Soul?
- Is there a particular individual who is helping me—and if so, how?
- Do you have any guidance about how I can realize my intention at this point in my life?

4. Use the Closing Prayer to exit your Records. If you haven't already done so, write down any information from your reading that you would like to recall in the future.

PART B

1. Use the Opening Prayer to access your Records again. Ask your Masters, Teachers, and Loved Ones to take you back to the Dimension of Choice. Then, ask the following questions about the family you're in right now:
   - What does it mean to me to honor my ancestors in this lifetime?
   - How can I expand the greatness of this particular ancestral line?
   - What contribution, or contributions, am I to make on behalf of this line's future descendants?

- How can I "reach into the future" and draw upon the power of these descendants right now?

2. Use the Closing Prayer to exit your Records. Write down any information from your reading that you would like to recall in the future.

EXERCISE

Identify and Clear Unwanted Ancestral Influences on the Present

1. Use the Opening Prayer to access your Records.

2. Ask your Masters, Teachers, and Loved Ones to help you see a limiting pattern that you "inherited" from your ancestors. Then, ask the following questions:
   - Where did this limiting pattern begin? What was the original intent behind it? What happened?
   - Is there any way in which this pattern is serving me and the highest probability of my ancestral line?
   - If this pattern no longer serves me, what will it take for me to evolve beyond it?
   - Which of my parents' ancestral lines holds the key to my freedom from this limiting pattern?

3. Use the Closing Prayer to exit your Records. Write down any information from your reading that you would like to recall in the future.

EXERCISE

Healing a Difficult Bond or Tie

1. Use the Opening Prayer to access your Records.

2. Ask your Masters, Teachers, and Loved Ones to show you a family member whom you find particularly troublesome. Then, ask these questions:
   - What are my family member and I working on in this ancestral line?
   - What is the true nature of the difficulty?
   - Why is it so difficult for me to accept this person as they are?
   - What happened between us that keeps us in this tension?
   - What Soul-level learning am I striving for in this situation?
   - How can I accept and make peace with this person so I can begin to heal the situation?
   - What is the highest probability of this relationship?

3. Use the Closing Prayer to exit your Records. Write down any information from your reading that you would like to recall in the future.

7

Healing Past Lives in the Akashic Records

Now that you've explored your ancestry to discover who you are today, the next chapter in the story of your Soul is to explore some of your past lives. Doing so will give you an even broader understanding of who you are today—and will provide another way to help your awareness of your Soul evolve.

Since the Akasha holds a record of *all* of our lifetimes, and because time and space as we know them do not exist in the Akashic Records, information regarding our problems and their origins is always readily available in the Records. Having said that, I want to make it clear that the Records do not function for us as The Big Fishing Pond in the Sky. We can't just open our Records, cast our line, and reel in information about our various past lives. The Lords of the Records allow only the Masters, Teachers, and Loved Ones to share information that we are ready to hear. So unless the problem a person is presenting began in a different lifetime, that person will not get past-life information during an Akashic Record reading. This may be frustrating to some of your clients who are especially intrigued by reincarnation. However, those who are well aware of divine timing and divine reliance will understand when it is and is not appropriate to receive information about past lives in the Records.

Past-life healing in the Records is similar to energy healing, in that your readings will follow different levels in order to help you:

- Explore past lives your Soul has lived
- Understand and release patterns of consciousness you developed during other lifetimes that no longer serve you in this one
- Align with the highest probabilities of your current lifetime in order to facilitate and expedite your Soul's evolution in its awareness of its Oneness with the Creator
- Recognize the countless ways you have demonstrated loving yourself throughout a variety of identities and circumstances

WHAT ARE PAST LIVES?

From an Akashic point of view, all Souls are eternal. Your Soul has been reincarnating throughout time to experience and express its divinity in a variety of conditions. The human lifetimes your Soul experienced before this current incarnation are known as your Soul's past lives. (The issue of moving from human form to animal form throughout the reincarnation cycle does not arise in the Akashic Records. Instead, we see only the journey of the Soul in its human incarnations. Whether a Soul transitions from human being to family pet is not addressed in the Records.)

At the start of each new lifetime, your Soul sets out to learn certain lessons and accomplish certain goals. In some cases, your Soul will learn a particular lesson within a single lifetime. At the end of such a lifetime, your Soul will shed its physical body and integrate the wisdom of that lesson into its consciousness. (In more familiar terms, this is when the body dies but the spirit lives on and is more evolved than ever because of its new understandings.)

Sometimes, however, a particular lesson takes more than one lifetime to master. In such a case, what once was merely a lesson to be learned at the human level becomes an energetic blockage or problem that must be cleared at the Soul level. Here's what happens.

Let's say your Soul enters a lifetime as "Katie," with a plan to work on overcoming prejudice. But this turns out to be a tall order, so despite Katie's best human efforts, she reaches the end of her lifetime without having mastered the lesson. As the human being known as Katie, your Soul made many advancements toward overcoming prejudice. Yet on this particular lesson, your Soul still has work to do. At the end of your lifetime as Katie, your Soul sheds Katie's physical body, but the energy of the unfinished lesson still exists as a blockage in your Soul-level consciousness. With nowhere else to go, this energy blockage takes up residence in the body and mind of your Soul's next incarnation, "Malik."

As Malik grows up, some of his prejudicial beliefs and actions are directly influenced by the unresolved problems Katie left behind. Malik's parents are baffled by his behavior. They can't understand how, despite the fact that they raised all of their children in the same way, Malik has such different ideas from the rest of his family. As a matter of fact, Malik himself doesn't always understand why he feels and acts as he does. There's just something deep down inside him that he can never quite explain.

In its lifetime as Katie, and now as Malik, your Soul has been allowed to view different kinds of prejudice through different sets of eyes in order to learn to overcome this problem. If your Soul succeeds during its lifetime as Malik, it will clear away the problem and its energy blockage, integrate the wisdom of the lesson, and move on to learn something else. However, if Malik does not succeed, your Soul might decide to come back as "Pierre" and try, try again.

This learning process will repeat itself for as many lifetimes as necessary for your Soul to solve its problem and integrate its lesson. Then, once the problem is solved, your Soul will be free to get on with the rest of its life—or more accurately, its lifetimes—unaffected any longer by this particular lesson and all of its resultant problems.

It is important to stop here and note that it is an energetic impossibility for a Soul to go backward in its evolution. A human experience may appear to be a regression to past patterns of thinking and behaving, but that does not mean the Soul is backsliding. Behaviors and ways of being that are constricting, limiting, and uncomfortable—criminal activity, addiction, extreme poverty, and violence, for example—are all valid paths for a Soul to take on its way to learning love and self-acceptance. They are opportunities to realize the Divine Presence, no matter what the circumstances. So do not be fooled by appearances; there is no going backward.

It can be especially difficult to reconcile this notion of choice with negative situations or old vestiges of reincarnation. From an Akashic perspective, which can be very different from other points of view, the purpose of reincarnation is to come to completely love and accept ourselves in any and all circumstances, no matter what. Eventually, over lifetimes, we expand that idea out into a widening circle. Each time we grow into the possibility of knowing and loving ourselves more, we take another step into knowing and loving others "as is" and finally loving the entirety of creation.

For some of us, myself included, the Akashic perspective is a very different idea of reincarnation from the one I originally learned—one which was based on a good/bad, right/wrong template that came with plenty of judgment and where the goal was to "zero out" at the end of all lifetimes. It can be very easy to know and love ourselves when we are wonderful and generous, but the story verges on downright upsetting if we are criminals, addicts, or poor. On the Akashic path, I am learning to love, accept, and appreciate myself and others no matter what.

Understanding this concept is similar to understanding the movement of a "retrograde" planet. Planets do not go backward, but they sometimes give the optical illusion of slowing down in their orbits, so much so that they appear to be going in reverse. Like those heavenly bodies in retrograde, in some lifetimes, we human "heavenly bodies" appear to be operating at a slower pace than others around us. Or we choose to live out a particularly difficult challenge that takes all of our focus and attention, so our progress appears to be minimal. But make no mistake, there is only progress in our Universe—always expanding, always unfolding, always evolving. Sometimes that evolution is easy to recognize, and sometimes it's unrecognizable.

HOW DOES PAST-LIFE HEALING OCCUR IN THE AKASHIC RECORDS?

Past-life healing in the Records is similar to energy healing in that both forms of healing follow the same three levels of telling your story, looking for the causes and conditions, and recognizing the Soul-level Truth. The differences in past-life healing, however, are that when you look for the causes and conditions of your problem during level two, your Masters, Teachers, and Loved Ones will help you meet with the past-life incarnation (person) that you were in the lifetime during which the problem originated. That past-life incarnation will then explain how and why the problem began and how you can heal it now. Then, when you look at the Soul-level Truth during level three, you will be given the opportunity to invite your past-life incarnation to either integrate itself into your Soul's consciousness or return to the Light of the Records.

As you might imagine, this is deep work in the Records. Attempt it only when you feel comfortable and ready to hear the information. When you *are* ready, you can use the following exercise to familiarize yourself with the process of healing past lives in the Records. Depending on your experiences during this exercise, you may or may not need to personally advance through all Three Levels of Healing. For the sake of learning the process, however, and knowing how to use all the levels for yourself and others in the future, you'll want to read through the entire exercise. When you use this exercise with another person, the three levels and the process will be identical, only you will be the one conducting the reading and facilitating the process.

EXERCISE

Working in the Akashic Records for Past-Life Healing

LEVEL 1: TELL YOUR STORY FROM YOUR POINT OF VIEW

1. During this level of healing, you will be working at the level of your problem and its physical manifestations. So think of a problem in your life that you haven't been able to resolve. Then, use the Opening Prayer to access your Akashic Records.

2. Begin this level by telling your story to your Masters, Teachers, and Loved Ones. (Write it down or say it out

loud, whichever is easier for you.) As you describe the problem from your perspective, include details, like how and when it started, who is involved, what impact it has had so far, and what complications it has caused.

3. While you are speaking or writing, pause every once in a while and decide whether you are being judgmental in any way. If you are, remind yourself that in this particular moment, you don't have a complete picture of the problem. Then, finish your story without judgment.

4. When you've finished telling your story, you're likely to sense a shift. It may feel like a sigh of relief, as if relating your problem without judgment has helped you get it off your chest—literally clear its heavy energy from your heart space—and you're starting to breathe a bit easier. You may also begin to see yourself and your problem from a broader, more compassionate perspective.

5. If talking about your problem was all that was necessary to clear its energy blockage, use the Closing Prayer to exit your Akashic Records.

Or:

If you still don't have a sense of resolution, keep your Records open and move into level two.

LEVEL 2: ASK ABOUT THE PAST-LIFE CAUSES AND CONDITIONS

1. Begin this part of the reading by asking your Masters, Teachers, and Loved Ones to help you establish a pillar of Light that will allow you the opportunity to meet with your Soul as it existed in a former lifetime. This pillar of Light will serve as your "Akashic meeting room." You'll be connected to the pillar by a bridge of Light that extends from your heart center to the pillar, about eighteen inches in front of you. Your Masters, Teachers, and Loved Ones will hold this space for the duration of the reading as a way of maintaining the separation between your Soul's current incarnation ("you") and its past-life incarnation. This separation will allow you to work in comfort and clarity. Once the pillar of Light is established, your Masters, Teachers, and Loved Ones will use it as the conduit through which all of the reading's energy, information, questions, and answers will flow.

2. Recall the problem you described during level one. Then, ask your Masters, Teachers, and Loved Ones to place in the pillar of Light the person you were in the lifetime during which your problem began.

3. In the presence of your Masters, Teachers, and Loved Ones, converse with your past-life incarnation. (Remember that your Masters, Teachers, and Loved Ones are holding that person in the Light and maintaining the space for you to do this work.) If you need help getting the conversation started, you might

ask the person's name. Then, you might ask any or all of these questions to learn more about your problem:
- What happened during your lifetime that caused the problem that I have now?
- How and why did this problem begin for you?
- What lesson was the problem meant to teach you?
- Why was it so difficult for you?
- Why am I still having trouble with the problem in this current lifetime?
- Is there something you can tell me that will help me view this problem in a way that will help me heal it?
- What else would you like me to know?
- I know I can't change what happened during your lifetime, but is there anything I can do for you now? Is there anything you need?
- What are the benefits of the choices you made that contribute positively to who you are then and throughout time?

4. During your conversation, keep asking yourself whether the information you're receiving is practical, useful, and pertinent. If it's not, ask the person to stay focused on your problem. If it is, keep going until you register the Aha moment that shifts your perspective and begins to move you toward healing.

5. After you experience that shift in perspective, you may feel like you got everything you needed and are ready to close your Records. Before you say the Closing Prayer, thank your Masters, Teachers, and Loved Ones for helping you explore this past life in order to learn the cause of your problem. Also thank the person who came forward from your past life to assist you

in your healing. Say goodbye, then count out loud: "One . . . two . . . THREE!" After you say, "THREE!" clap your hands once. This will both let that person go and disperse the blocked energy your Soul had been carrying because of the problem. Clapping will also disperse the pillar of Light as well as your bridge to it.

6. Use the Closing Prayer to exit your Records.

Or:

If you're having trouble making peace with the person you were—or with what the person did—during that former lifetime, keep your Records open and move into level three.

LEVEL 3: RECOGNIZE THE SOUL-LEVEL TRUTH

1. Remember that you are still in your Records, and that the pillar of Light that your Masters, Teachers, and Loved Ones established at the beginning of level two is still in place. Now, ask your Masters, Teachers, and Loved Ones to help you shift your altitude of consciousness until you are able to see your past-life incarnation from the perspective of the Akashic Records. Regardless of what that person appeared to be or do, ask to see their true essence in the Light of the Records. Ask to replace any judgment of that human with love for their—for your—eternal Soul. Ask to replace the illusion of being separate from that person with the recognition of your Oneness. Ask to stop rejecting that part of your Soul and embrace it with compassion instead.

2. If necessary, speak with your past-life incarnation some more. Ask it to show you how it did its best, and love it for its human efforts. Embrace its divine spark as the Truth of its essence, and stop rejecting its earthly form.

3. Now, ask your Masters, Teachers, and Loved Ones to expand your heart center so you can invite your past-life incarnation into your heart. Make room within yourself for that expression of yourself, and enfold it in your heart's embrace. Then, ask your past-life incarnation if it would like to stay and integrate itself into your Soul's consciousness, or if it would like to leave and go back into the pillar of Light. Whatever it decides to do will be the best way for you to achieve healing, so trust that what it chooses is for the highest good of all.

4. If your past-life incarnation decides to integrate, ask your Masters, Teachers, and Loved Ones to assist in this process. If it decides to return to the Light, say goodbye and let it go as you count to three and clap. When you finish, the energy of your problem will be dispersed, and the pillar of Light and your bridge to it will be dispersed as well.

5. Use the Closing Prayer to exit your Records.

Normally, following these three levels of past-life healing is enough to dislodge most problems and clear their energy blockages. If you have a problem that's particularly challenging, continually ask yourself: *How do I love myself in the midst of this pain or unresolved situation?* You can go into your Records and repeat this process as many times as you need to until you find clarity and peace. It may also be true that you had other past lives that play into this particular problem. If that's the case, when you get to level two, ask to be shown a different lifetime during which this same problem existed, and converse with another of your Soul's incarnations to get their perspective. As always, make sure that the information you receive is practical, useful, and pertinent. If it's not, you are free at any time to end the reading by counting to three, clapping your hands, and closing your Akashic Records.

The most important thing to remember while doing this healing work is that you are the authority when it comes to determining your own experiences. In other words, you are the one who will know whether a problem is cleared or needs more work. You also will know how much you can handle at any given time, so it's up to you to set your own comfortable pace. There is no need to rush the process. Actually, doing so can have a negative effect that further complicates things. So be your own spiritual authority. Take the information you receive from your Masters, Teachers, and Loved Ones and use it to determine your best strategy for healing.

EXPLORING POSITIVE PAST LIVES IN THE AKASHIC RECORDS

Though exploring past lives is extremely helpful for healing existing problems, there are also times when exploring past lives can support you in situations that are already good. For example, let's say you've been made a manager at work. While you're thrilled with this vote of confidence in your ability and expertise, you're also kind of nervous. Being promoted to this new position involves a lot of unknowns. You wish you had a mentor, someone who's "been there and done that" before, who can give you some pointers as you begin to navigate your new position.

Well, guess what? You *do* have a mentor; it's you! That is, it's "you" as you were in a past life during which you were an expert at managing others. All you have to do to receive that past-life expert's advice is go into your Records and ask for it.

You can use the following exercise to explore a positive past life in your Records. The process you will follow is a simplified version of the process you used for past-life healings. If you choose to explore a positive past life while reading for someone else, you can use the following process and rephrase the questions as necessary.

EXERCISE

Exploring Positive Past-Life Experiences

1. Think of a situation about which you would like the knowledge and advice of a "past-life expert." Then, use the Opening Prayer to access your Akashic Records.

2. Ask your Masters, Teachers, and Loved Ones to help you establish a pillar of Light that will allow you the opportunity to meet with your Soul as it existed in a former lifetime. This pillar of Light will serve as your "Akashic meeting room." You'll be connected to the pillar by a bridge of Light that extends from your heart center to the pillar, about eighteen inches in front of you. Your Masters, Teachers, and Loved Ones will hold this space for the duration of the reading as a way of maintaining the separation between your Soul's current incarnation ("you") and its past-life incarnation. This separation will allow you to work in comfort and clarity. Once the pillar of Light is established, your Masters, Teachers, and Loved Ones

will use it as the conduit through which all of the reading's energy, information, questions, and answers will flow.

3. Recall the issue about which you are seeking advice. Then, ask your Masters, Teachers, and Loved Ones to place in the pillar of Light the person you were in a past life who can best help with the issue at hand.

4. In the presence of your Masters, Teachers, and Loved Ones, converse with your past-life incarnation. (Remember that your Masters, Teachers, and Loved Ones are holding that person in the Light and are maintaining the space for you to do this work.) If you need help getting the conversation started, you might ask the person's name. Then, you might ask some of these questions or come up with some of your own:
   - What happened during your lifetime that caused you to be so successful?
   - What qualities do you possess that contributed to your success?
   - If any of those qualities are latent in me, how can I cultivate and use them?
   - Are there any pitfalls you can help me avoid?
   - What other pertinent advice or information would you like to give me?
   - In your expert opinion, what can I do to ensure my earthly success in the future?
   - How can my Soul achieve maximum growth from this situation?

5. During your conversation, keep asking yourself whether the information you're receiving is practical, useful, and pertinent. If it's not, ask the person to stay focused on your issue. If it is, keep going until you register the Aha moment that shifts your perspective and moves you into greater understanding.

6. When you sense that your conversation is coming to a close, you can do one of two things:
   - You can invite your past-life incarnation to integrate into your consciousness.

Or:

   - You can thank your past-life incarnation for assisting you in your learning and send them back to the Light. If this is your choice, say goodbye and count out loud: "One . . . two . . . THREE!" After you say, "THREE!" clap your hands one time to let the person go.

7. Use the Closing Prayer to exit your Records.

The preceding past-life exercises work just the same whether you're exploring your own positive past lives or are helping other people explore theirs. The results will vary depending on each person's receptivity and level of understanding. However, in every case, as we learned with "Joe" in chapter 5, the healing will have begun on some level, even if it's not obvious right away.

As you'll discover after working in your Akashic Records for a time, there are many healing methods and avenues to explore. Given that this is a beginning-level book, I've presented the methods that I feel will provide the most solid foundation for you. They can serve as a powerful springboard that will help you dive into your personal journey of spiritual healing and growth. When you feel confident with these concepts, advance yourself to the next level with my book *Healing Through the Akashic Records*.

8

Life with the Akashic Records

What I've learned from working in the Akashic Records is that they have their own perspective, which provides an ever-expanding view of my Soul's ever-unfolding essence. Once I became accustomed to that perspective—to that altitude of awareness, or consciousness—I recognized that working in the Records is a radical opportunity to view myself and my whole life from a very different angle. I also began to realize some basic Truths, which I call my Akashic Assumptions. From a Records point of view, these things are assumed to be true for every Soul, all of the time. While I have numbered them for clarity here, please know that they are listed in no particular order, as they are of equal importance!

AKASHIC ASSUMPTIONS

1. **There's always more than meets the (human) eye.**
   From the human perspective of a single lifetime, certain

people and events can appear nasty, horrible, wrong—even devastating, as is the case with such natural disasters as hurricanes, tsunamis, and earthquakes. And they really are horrible. Yet from the eternal perspective of the Akashic Records, there's always more than meets the eye—reasons we don't understand and ultimate benefits we don't see. Even though this is true, the Masters, Teachers, and Loved Ones never minimize our human suffering. Instead they offer suggestions to not only work through a difficult situation, but to understand its karmic value. With their help, we can learn the meaning of our suffering, and we can grow from it. And eventually, from a Soul-level perspective, we might come to see that absolutely all events, and all of the people involved, are doing their parts in providing opportunities for growth, clarity, purpose, and healing. We see instances of this all around us. After floodwaters submerge a city, for instance—taking lives, destroying homes, and crippling businesses—the city's residents reach out to each other to help rebuild and repair, while officials band together to find ways to improve the city's infrastructure. Or as another example, an innocent child is killed in the crossfire of a gang shooting. This shocks the entire neighborhood. Yet after mourning their heartbreaking loss, the neighbors galvanize: They hold prayer vigils and town meetings, they organize a neighborhood watch, and they beautify their streets and parks. And eventually, their neighborhood becomes a better place to live.

So despite the initial pain and loss that some people or events can cause, the Akashic Records will show us how even the most devastating circumstances provide opportunities for transformation in which a larger purpose emerges—one that helps us see beyond individual needs to the need of the unified whole to experience its innate goodness. When we view events this way, we can see why it appears that "bad things happen to good people." In truth, these events are not personal at all, and no person or thing is "good" or "bad." The eternal perspective negates good and bad. This means no person or group is ever singled out for punishment, payback, or karmic retribution (see Assumption #6). Instead, these brave Souls and Soul-groups are actually enduring their situations to elevate the consciousness of the planet.

2. **We are all One.**

All humans exist within the absolute Oneness. We cannot escape who we already are or opt out of our Soul's journey. In other words, there is no such thing as being outside of, or disconnected from, the Oneness. There is only the state of becoming aware of your existence within the Whole. So from an Akashic perspective, all Souls are on their way to discovering that we are One, connected by—and contained within—the loving Light of life itself.

3. **Everything and everyone is an expression of spiritual, unconditional, or Divine Love.**

Not only are we all One, our inner essence is purely Divine Love—earthly appearances sometimes to the contrary. If we're in the Akashic Records and we look long enough, we will find the essence of unconditional love—that point of Light and goodness—within absolutely every Soul in existence. Within the Records, it is easier to discern the spiritual aspect and innate goodness of everyone and every experience. This is a decisively different way to view ourselves and the world. We begin to sense everything and everyone as some expression of unconditional love. Key questions include: *How does this situation empower me/my client to have a direct experience of my/their goodness? How can I love now? In what ways am I doing this to expand my experience of love?*

4. **Everyone is always in active pursuit of peace and committed to expanding their personal experience of love.**

   From an Akashic perspective, absolutely everyone wants to live in a state of peace, love, and goodness, and will go to great lengths to achieve it. From a human perspective, some people's attempts at achieving peace make little or no sense. Hitler, Stalin, Trump, and many other leaders around the globe have been, in their own minds, so committed to securing their own peace, emotional safety, and love that they destroy the same qualities of others. Though their methods appear quite awful in the eyes of most of the world, from an Akashic point of view, even those Souls were (and are) on their way to awakening to their own essential goodness and recognizing their connection to the Oneness. It just takes some Souls more lifetimes to learn compassionate paths to more safety, security, and love. This does not mean, however, that they won't get there. Eventually, every Soul does.

5. **Reincarnation is not about "good" and "bad" lifetimes.**

   As I have come to understand reincarnation from an altitude of consciousness, I have realized that it is not about "good" and "bad" lifetimes—a lifetime of crime versus a lifetime of philanthropy, for example. Instead, reincarnation is about the journey that a particular Soul chooses to take in order to become aware of itself on the physical plane. This journey on the physical plane allows the Soul to come to know itself as divine, spiritual, and good—to grow in its awareness of itself over an expanse of different lifetimes and in a variety of contexts.

6. **The question before each Soul is always:** *How do I love myself now, even when my behavior is terrible? How is this an opportunity to expand my experience of being safe, loved, and good?*
   As a Soul comes to know itself, it is graced with multiple opportunities to learn compassion and love for itself as well as other Souls. So in its lifetime as a "criminal," for example, that Soul has a unique and powerful opportunity to dissolve the false barriers that exist in its own understanding of its goodness. It can come to understand that the barrier is in the perception, and that the behavior comes out of that perception. (In other words, how that *Soul* thinks it knows itself in that lifetime will determine how it chooses to act.) But the more enlightened that Soul becomes, the more aware it becomes of the absolute Truth that it is a physical expression of infinite Light and love, and it is free to be generous and loving. Such a realization can happen in a single lifetime, as in the case of the hardened criminal who "comes to see the Light." Alternatively, it can happen over the course of several lifetimes. Either way, it's okay. Since time as we know it does not exist in the Records, and all Souls are eternal, we have all the "time"—and lifetimes—we need.

7. **Karma is not about reward and punishment.**
   Having learned that reincarnation is the journey of all Souls that leads to ultimate goodness and Oneness, I have also discovered that karma has no punitive aspect. Rather, karma is a series of cause-and-effect relationships that allow

us opportunities to discover what can result when we make different choices. In the Akashic Records, the basis for evaluation is always grounded in compassion. The Masters, Teachers, and Loved Ones never judge our actions; they merely help us understand them. They know we are becoming our potential, and they don't clobber us because we're not there yet. Instead, they reveal both the motivating factors that preceded our actions and the outcomes that most likely will follow them. It is then (and always) up to us to choose the action we will take next. What results from that action will create our karma. It won't be good; it won't be bad. It will just *be*.

Without the notion of karma as reward and punishment, we are free to view ourselves with acceptance and understanding. So from the vantage point of the Records, I can say with absolute certainty that I am a human being who's becoming increasingly aware of my innate goodness and "Godness." At this moment, and in all moments, I am completely loving and whole; I just don't always remember that fact. But I'm working on it! And what I see when I look through the eyes of the Records precludes any need for forgiveness because there is no condemnation.

What is always required is acceptance, which sidesteps the question and challenge of forgiveness. Forgiveness implies judgment, which is the source of our dilemma, given that we are not the authorities. Without judgment, we are left with a simple matter of acceptance, which recognizes the reality (but not necessarily approval) of the existence of a person or behavior. With acceptance, we can relinquish our opinions and let go of old ideas. New, more loving possibilities emerge. Negative judgments, opinions, and perspectives cause cycles of cause and effect to repeat—a painful process that can be resolved through acceptance. What we have come to know as "stuck karma" can be resolved with acceptance.

Finally, there is only an exquisite love story: the story of my Soul's existence. Though the journey has, at times, been filled with terrible hardship and struggle, it has been graced in equal measure with unspeakable richness and love. And always, all along the journey, as I continue to catch glimpses of my true self in the eyes of other Souls, I fall more deeply in love with the Oneness that we are. I recognize that every action I ever took, every cherished idea, was my best effort to expand my personal experience of being loved. The question to consistently ask is: *How do I love myself now?* How grateful I am to be alive in this moment, viewing the world from this altitude of awareness. How beautiful we all appear in the Light of the Akashic Records!

THE AKASHIC ABSOLUTES

The shorthand version of everything I've just said is something I call "The Akashic Absolutes": Fear Not, Judge Not, and Resist Not. These are the guidelines by which our Masters, Teachers, and Loved Ones would have us live our lives—if they had the choice.

I realize these can seem like a tall order, so remember that this life is a journey. We fear *less* on our way to Fear Not. We judge *less* on the path to Judge Not. We resist *less* until we Resist Not. Here is how it works.

Fear Not

After working in the Akashic Records for a while, we begin to relax because we can see that every situation that ever existed either has been or will be resolved for the highest good of all. It may not happen today or even in this lifetime, yet every issue does indeed result in peace and goodness. The game of life won't end until we Souls achieve this shared goal.

We also can see that there is a part of us that is indestructible, that nothing can obliterate, that lives on forever. We see that we have had lifetimes of terrible poverty, war, natural disasters, human cruelty—and yet we are still intact. The essence of who we are is immutable. Nothing can separate us from the essential goodness within us, and as we come to know this as real and true, fear begins to fall away until there is nothing left to fear.

Judge Not

From a Records point of view, we begin to see that we are not the judges of the Universe, not the judges of others, and not even the judges of ourselves! Really! We begin to see all people, including ourselves, growing into their own awareness, developing their own authority, and making determinations on their own behalf. It becomes abundantly clear to us that other people are quite capable, and we can trust them with their own lives and decisions. We are not "in charge" or in any position of authority over others sufficiently enough to judge them.

Of course, we still make choices for ourselves, for this is the only place we have authority and power. Other people get to make their own choices, even if we don't agree with them. When that happens, all we can do is choose to participate with them or not. Either way, the only thing we can "judge" is what is appropriate for us.

When we begin to recognize that every action, choice, and decision we (and others) make is our best effort to experience love, we can begin to let go of our need to judge. As we accept this idea and let go of judgment, the world becomes a safe and beautiful place.

Resist Not

If there is not a reason to judge and there is nothing to fear, then the only thing left not to do is resist what makes us uncomfortable.

The causes of discomfort vary greatly from person to person and lifetime to lifetime. Some people may be uncomfortable with conflicts in relationships or even too much success. Other people may be uncomfortable with humiliation or shameful behavior. Whatever the reason, when we resist and push away from what makes us uncomfortable, we begin to build an energetic wall that keeps growing all around us until the very thing we resist becomes the barrier that keeps us from moving through it.

Resistance is a rejection. If I am resisting a part of myself, I am rejecting that part of myself. If I am resisting a person or what that person is trying to give me, I am rejecting all or part of that person. If I don't resist but just let something be, it will go its merry way. For example, if I resist my hurt feelings about something, they will build up around and inside me and block me from moving through them. However, if I can just *be* with my hurt feelings, I can eventually let them go and make room for different feelings.

The importance of practicing The Akashic Absolutes is to give yourself a chance to grow more deeply in the Records. Proceed at a pace that feels comfortable. Take one step and one situation at a time, and ask for help when you need it. As you apply what you've been given, more will come to you. The idea is to grow into the infinite Light, not to be overwhelmed or blinded by it.

FINAL THOUGHTS ON THE AKASHIC RECORDS: THE PAST, THE PRESENT . . . AND THE FUTURE

Earlier, I explained that the Akashic Records contain the story of your Soul over lifetimes, and that this current incarnation has its own unique story. But what about the future? The possibilities and probabilities of your future are held in your Records too.

We see the deepest meaning and truest value of the Records in how we use them to support and guide us as we move into our future. As you apply that guidance and rely on the energy of the Records, your own future will take the form of the life you've always wanted. Not every detail will be the same as you had first envisioned it, but the general direction and quality of your life will match your original intentions. So if you have been desiring a life of adventure, you will have it. If you have wanted a life of passion, it will be yours. Whatever your Soul has been seeking, you eventually will find it, simply because you can only desire that which is already yours. Because this dream lives within you, the dream itself signals that you already have within you all you need to make it come true.

You will grow more and more into your own personal heaven on earth. Will it be a life without challenges, obstacles, and stress? Of course not. It will be a human life with physical occurrences, mental activities, and emotional upheaval. Yet you will live it from a place of grace so that as circumstances unfold, you, my friend and new Akashic practitioner, will discover that you are able to be happy, kind, respectful, and generous, even when things aren't going your way. The more you use the Records, the more you'll be able to enjoy the life you have. Your life will continue to become more and more of what you've always wanted.

Something else I want you to know is that as the Light in you shines brighter than ever before, your soulmates and traveling companions will find you. It will be so much easier for you to recognize those like-minded, like-spirited Souls, and you'll have a wonderful time together. When you meet for the first time in person, it will seem like a reunion of longtime friends. And do you know what? That's exactly what it will be!

I want to acknowledge you for responding to the inner prompting that urged you to pick up this book. It is a courageous and beautiful step to honor the call of your Soul and set your feet upon the path. Know that you are never alone, never lost. Just open your Akashic Records and ask for help. Though your

Masters, Teachers, and Loved Ones will never intrude, they are always happy to help. If you share the Records with your friends, you can be there for each other in remarkable and powerful ways. On your own, you will become a strong Light. But together, you will be a focal point of vital, brilliant Light.

We are living in a fascinating time. What distinguishes our age from all others is the fact that individuals are now able to take responsibility for their own understanding and their relationship with their own spiritual authority. This is a liberating notion for individuals, and it is potentially dangerous to the status quo.

Throughout history, humanity has been growing into the idea that it has "say" or authority over itself. We have been wrestling with ideas of our relationship to authority, both human and divine, for centuries. The movement toward responsible participation has been gaining momentum for the past few centuries, exemplified by the political revolutions in the United States (1775) and France (1789).

Today, we are moving beyond the age of national identity to the age of Oneness, or the global village. This has been facilitated by the brilliant, sophisticated technology that has been made available in the past twenty years. In the United States, the degree of political participation is greater than at any other time in our history and is more inclusive of the various segments of the population. On one hand, we are teetering on the edge of disaster; on the other, we are poised to launch into an age of possibilities beyond our wildest dreams. There is general agreement that our old ideas are no longer working and that our entire planet is suffering from our limited sense of connection to earth and our narrow sense of responsibility for its well-being. On a collision course with global disaster in every area—economics, politics, health care, and the distribution of resources—we can no longer afford the luxury of self-centeredness. We are face-to-face with our fears of standing up for ourselves and others in the presence of greed, and we are just beginning to get the idea that we *do* make a difference, and that no one else is going to rescue us from our mounting problems. It is occurring to us that we have a role to play in the well-being of our world.

Spiritually, we have relied upon institutions, organizations, and even our own minds to give us the sense of power we have wanted. We have believed that if we could just sort everything out and find our way with our well-trained minds, we could tap into the pipeline of spiritual aliveness we know exists. But this has failed. *Thinking* about spirituality has not empowered us. We have certainly learned a lot, but the illusion that we could access spiritual power through our minds has collapsed. We have followed the rules and precepts of both Eastern and Western religions, and these have been a helpful start. They have not, however, provided the catalyst that we had hoped would propel us into direct access of spiritual power. The age of keeping our heads down and our mouths shut is over. The day of waiting for someone stronger, better, and smarter to come along and figure things out is over. The hope of one leader coming onto the scene and taking the helm to steer us out of the morass will not be satisfied. We are clear that the old way does not work. It has been successful up to a point, but it cannot take us into the experience of spiritual power that we can use in our everyday lives. The heartening news is that the Akashic Records *can*.

The significance of the Pathway Prayer Process to Access the Heart of the Akashic Records is that it is a spiritual means into a spiritual dimension that holds energy, power, and wisdom. The Pathway Prayer takes us into the Heart of this dimension so energy (power) and information (wisdom) can inform and direct the mind and the will. The mind is wonderful, yet it has not been what we hoped it would be for humanity: It does not have the sensitivity or compassion that real people need. Knowledge is essential, yet without the heart's guidance, it is incomplete.

The will is critical to manifesting and realizing the ideas of the mind. Yet without the heart, the will can be cold and ruthless; if the heart does not have its say, the will can manifest results that are ultimately unsatisfying.

At this point in the history of human spiritual development, it is time for individuals to have direct access to spiritual resources. The Pathway Prayer Process provides direct access to the spiritual resource of the Akashic Records, and this book is the training tool you need to cultivate your relationship with spiritual power. This is a new idea. It is rooted in the awareness that no one person carries the potential to transform our lives for us. This new understanding is that each of us has the same Light within, and no one can do our part for us—that only I can do my part, and only you can do your part. We can no longer wait for anyone outside ourselves to get us out of our dilemmas and into the flow of the spiritual life force, whether on a personal level or a global one.

For the first time in the history of humanity, everyone is being called to wake up to a new and wonderful opportunity and participate to the best of their ability. Participation is now self-determined. I can join in if I want to. No one else decides for me. Participation is no longer based on gender, race, or class. Taking responsibility and doing one's part is based on individual choice. Each one of us can see what needs to be done and has the grace within to do it. I have within me the ability and energy to do my individual part. I do not have the ability or the energy to do your part, however. Likewise, you don't have what it takes to do my part, but you have exactly what's required to do what you do best. This is a fabulous system, and it's directly related to the Akashic Records being available to anyone who wants to access them. Deep within all human beings is a clear and profound sense of our essence. It may be buried under all kinds of unresolved issues and fears, yet rest assured, it's there. The Akashic Records provide a way to be in conscious, direct relationship with this presence in an intimate and manageable format. The Records are being opened to non-clerical people like you and me who are the hope of the future.

Humanity has been crying out for help for a very long time. Help was given first to religious leaders, then to political and economic leaders and external organizations. But in the hands of these "others," significant global change has not yet occurred. This is because global change must begin with individuals, and it must come from within. The transmission and activation of global change begins when one Soul recognizes the Light in another. Across the planet, one Soul at a time, "pockets" of individual points of Light have begun to form. As these pockets of Light continue to recognize each other, they will form a "blanket" of Light that will eventually converge and cover the entire planet, radiating the best of who we are and magnetizing the best in those around us. This Light meeting Light will transform our reality.

This movement of inner spiritual awareness is already underway and will continue until each and every person is seen in the Truth of who they are. As this Light spreads, it will form a layer of Light-consciousness of goodwill, peace, and harmony that will support all our human efforts to have life work in every way, for everyone.

You, dear reader, have been drawn to this book by an inner prompting. It is no accident that you now hold it in your hands. There is something already active within you that brought you to this movement. The Lords of the Records are beckoning you to begin the transformation you seek. Your Masters, Teachers, and Loved Ones are waiting to provide you with all the energetic backing and wisdom you need to realize your incredible potential. This is your time, right now.

We are in a transitional generation. Our parents did not know about personal responsibility in the way we know it now, nor did they ever consider having direct access to their own spiritual authority—well, some did, but their generation as a whole did not. The Akashic Records were not widely available until now because there had to be enough development of the mass consciousness to be able to handle this resource. Now that has happened. We have seen an explosion in meditation, heart-mind connection work, personal healing, and Light healing for ourselves and others. All of these practices have enabled the masses to mature sufficiently to be ready to use the Akashic Records in the best ways for personal growth and global healing. Our children might not need a tool like this. They might take it for granted and assume that they are entitled to receive insight and support from the spiritual resource of their choosing. We are the generation that needs the training. We are the Bridge of Light. As we construct this bridge with the Pathway Prayer Process, we make it easier for those who come after us. Our descendants will find it the most natural thing in the world to be in direct, conscious relationship with their Soul and its corresponding expression in the Universe.

And so, my friends, thank you so much for stepping onto your path, along with so many others who are committed to walking in the Light of Truth, the Light of peace, the Light of power, and the Light of love. We stand together, shoulder to shoulder, moving ahead in our ordinary lives with an extra-ordinary perspective. You are a point of Light within an amazing, infinite Light that permeates all of life and every Soul in the Universe. I want you to know that I know there is a Light that only you can shine. I know that your Light is unique and vital to the illumination of humanity. Together, our Lights will shine and brighten the path for all who choose to join. You will know when the time is right for you; and when that moment arrives, you will set your feet upon the path. And together, we will do what we could never do alone.

Much love and many blessings,
Linda Howe

Gratitude

Sharing this journey with other seekers like you is my life's joy! Thank you to each and every person who stepped on this path of spiritual awareness, whether for a few moments, years, or lifetimes. Your participation has made a positive, discernible difference in the quality of my life and the lives of those I've had the honor of teaching.

Special thanks to the "A" Team. Enjoying this amazing Akashic Adventure with you has been fabulous and fun! Jean Lachowicz, Susan Lucci, Cindy Waldon, and Mr. Brian Fischer—charter members of the "A" Team! I love you all and am eternally grateful for all you have done, are doing, and will continue to do for the work.

Thanks so much to all the gracious and wonderful people at Sounds True. I am profoundly grateful that you reached out to me in 2009, willing to learn this method and put this work in front of your audience. When *How to Read the Akashic Records* was first released in 2009, there were no other books about the Akasha on the market. You trusted me to introduce the Realm of the Akasha to everyone. I'll always be grateful for this wonderful opportunity to further my life's work and inspire so many Souls.

To my siblings, one and all, thank you!

Finally, to my soulmate and partner, Lisa. My deepest gratitude for sharing this walk with me, staying the course, keeping the faith and focus, and knowing that this is my regular job. And to Michael, the most remarkable son in the Universe, you are the best. I love you both.

Further Resources

Please visit lindahowe.com to learn how to work in the Akashic Records. The Linda Howe Center for Akashic Studies offers a comprehensive course of study designed to help you bring your Soul's purposes to life.

In addition to the other works of Dr. Howe, we recommend exploring:

Chaney, Robert. *Akashic Records: Past Lives & New Directions.* Astara, 2009.

Dowling, Levi H. *The Aquarian Gospel of Jesus the Christ.* DeVorss & Company, 1997.

Laszlo, Ervin. *Science and the Akashic Field: An Integral Theory of Everything.* Inner Traditions, 2007.

Todeschi, Kevin J. *Edgar Cayce on the Akashic Records: The Book of Life.* A.R.E. Press, 1998.

Appendix

The Pathway Prayer Process to Access the Heart of the Akashic Records

TO OPEN YOUR OWN AKASHIC RECORDS:
- Say lines 1–10 of the Opening Prayer aloud, inserting "myself" or "me" as appropriate.
- Repeat lines 8–10 silently two more times.
- Announce the opening of the Records by saying line 11 aloud.

TO OPEN THE RECORDS OF ANOTHER PERSON:
- Say lines 1–5 of the Opening Prayer aloud.
- Say lines 6–7 silently one time.
- Say lines 8–10 aloud one time, inserting the person's first name.
- Repeat lines 8–10 silently two more times, inserting the person's current legal name or "her/him/them" as appropriate.
- Announce the opening of the Records by saying line 11 aloud.

TO CLOSE THE RECORDS:
Read the Closing Prayer aloud.

Opening Prayer

1. And so we do acknowledge the Forces of Light,

2. Asking for guidance, direction, and courage to know the Truth

3. as it is revealed for our highest good and the highest good of

4. everyone connected to us.

5. Oh, Holy Spirit of God,

6. Protect me from all forms of self-centeredness

7. and direct my attention to the work at hand.

8. Help me to know *(myself/first name of individual being read)* in the Light of the Akashic Records,

9. To see *(myself/first name of individual being read)* through the eyes of the Lords of the Records,

10. And enable me to share the wisdom and compassion that the Masters, Teachers, and Loved Ones of *(me/first name of individual being read)* have for *(me/them)*.

11. The Records are now open.

Closing Prayer

I would like to thank the Masters, Teachers, and Loved Ones for their love and compassion.

I would like to thank the Lords of the Akashic Records for their point of view.

And I would like to thank the Holy Spirit of Light for all knowledge and healing.

The Records are now closed. Amen.
The Records are now closed. Amen.
The Records are now closed. Amen.

Glossary of Akashic Terms

For easy access, I have gathered terms you may encounter while working in the Akashic Records.

Akasha: *All that is*; the primary substance from which everything originates. Energy in its first and earliest state—before it has been directed by our thoughts and affected by our emotions in this lifetime.

Akashic Absolutes, The—Fear Not, Judge Not, Resist Not: These are the governing principles of the Akasha, which, together, safeguard the culture of infinite kindness, dignity, and respect. As we become accustomed to identifying the Light and good in all, we see that there is nothing to fear. This frees us to stop judging, knowing that there is an essentially beneficial concept underlying everything that exists, leaving us no reason to resist. Since the Light and goodness of our Soul cannot be decimated by any person or situation, as we come to know our own eternal, infinite, unlimited spiritual nature, we can relinquish fear and resistance.

Akashic Record reading: Time and attention dedicated to encountering the Akashic Field consciously, responsibly, and deliberately for the purpose of expanding awareness of Soul-level Truths and the Divine Reality. This activity can be done for oneself or on behalf of another with their express permission. An Akashic Record reading affords the opportunity to sense and see who we are, presenting life challenges from the infinite, merciful perspective of the Soul. Everyone is a Soul that's fully entitled to a more conscious relationship with this dimension of self.

Akashic Records: The Soul-level dimension of consciousness, containing a vibrational Record of every Soul and its journey. It exists everywhere in its entirety and is completely available at all times and in all places. As such, the Records are an experiential body of knowledge that contains everything that every Soul has ever thought, said, and done over the course of its existence, as well as all its future possibilities.

Beings of Light (also Light Being): Unseen entities entrusted with the flow of operations within the Records, and between the Records and us mortal human beings.

Forces of Light: An alliance of all infinite, eternal, imminent Light Beings from all dimensions of this Universe, gathered to reinforce the accessibility of Light to humans in transmittable, receivable, useful form.

God: *All that is;* the author of the Universe. Everyone has the right to a god of their understanding, no matter what name is used (Source, the Divine, Divine Reality, and so on).

Heart of the Akashic Records: The Records' most powerful location, which facilitates integrating the Heart, mind, and will so we can operate in both the Records and the world as fully synthesized beings.

Lords of the Records: The collective of nonphysical Light Beings who have never been human and are responsible for maintaining the integrity and incorruptibility of the Akashic Records. They decide who may access the Records and what information will be revealed during a particular reading. They work in a group and do not reveal their individual identities or engage with individual humans. Their primary focus is the sanctity of the Akasha and effective transmission of energies to the Masters.

Loved Ones: People we have known in this lifetime, now deceased, who are committed to the awakening of our Souls. These relationships are not necessarily personality-based and may be as simple as a sense of someone from our present life, now dead, who seemed to have an uncanny ability to see us, know us, and connect with the Light in our eyes. Though they prefer not to be identified, they will reveal themselves during a reading if they feel that us knowing they are around will support us in that moment. They do not do the reading, and we do not channel them within the Akasha. Often, when someone we love passes on, we have a sense that they are somehow comforting and encouraging us from the other side. The optimal role of the Loved Ones inspires us to dignity.

Masters: Like the Lords of the Records, they are a group of non-physical Light Beings who do not identify personally or relate directly with humans. However, they work with individuals. Your particular group of Masters has been with you since your Soul's inception, for all time, and is responsible for the expansion of your awareness of your Soul's perfection through the human experience. They call upon just the right Teachers and Loved Ones who are best suited to help you as your journey unfolds and your developmental needs change.

Past Lives: From an Akashic point of view, all Souls are eternal. The human lifetimes your Soul experienced before this current incarnation are known as your Soul's Past Lives. Past Lives refer to your personal identities in other times and places.

Pillars of Light/Consciousness: Consciousness concepts consisting of incarnation, authority, discipline, responsibility, commitment, and grace. The first five concepts are identified by a precise vibration of Light, yet within the entire body of Light, they operate as a unit: Each pillar forms one point of the five-pointed star. Your interpretation of these five concepts determines the quality of your functioning in the world. Grace resides in the star's central pillar.

Reincarnation: At the beginning of each new lifetime, your Soul sets out to expand awareness of its essential goodness, the goodness of all others, and life itself, no matter what appearances suggest. Through a series of a variety of lifetimes, as a number of differing human identities, you have the opportunity to learn to love and accept who you are in any and all circumstances, as you are known and loved by the Divine. Sometimes a particular aspect of this growth may take more than one lifetime to master. Through a series of human lives, you come to know and love who you are in limited mortal form and love others and all of life, which is the ultimate purpose of the journey of all Souls.

Soul: That essential, reflective dimension of being that knows its Divine Nature, enjoys connection with the wholeness of Light and life, and yet expresses a distinct individual facet of the whole. A Soul's Divine Nature is infinite, eternal, unlimited, and simultaneously imminent and intimate. This aspect of being assumes human form through a series of lifetimes for the purpose of awakening to exaltation while in limited, finite, mortal human form.

Spirit: The Spirit of God, One, All That Is, Great Mystery—distinct from any individualized personality or personification of the God Force or Divine Presence.

Teachers: Teachers may or may not have been incarnate and, like the Masters, work in groups without sharing descriptive information about themselves. They prefer to remain unidentified so as not to foster personal dependence upon them. Their tenure is lesson-specific: They stay with us only for as long as it takes to absorb a particular understanding and integrate the consciousness into everyday human application. Teachers are specialists in concepts, such as self-trust, unconditional love, and appropriate communication, and may include major world teachers.

Zone of Choice: A particular realm we visit with our Masters, Teachers, and Loved Ones within the Records to make choices in between incarnations.

Questions and Answers about the Akashic Records

HOW ARE THE RECORDS ORGANIZED?

Q. Where is the Akashic Field located?
A. The location of the Akasha is everywhere! Yes, it is held within our atomic structure and, at the same time, holds our atoms. It is fully, wholly present everywhere and anywhere. So it can be accessed anywhere in the world.

Q. How do you know that you are not in the astral plane and not receiving information from astral entities? My friend is an Akashic Records reader and often talks about her confusion in this situation.
A. First, when working in the Records, you are nowhere near the astral plane (a nonphysical realm where angels and Souls in between incarnations are believed by some to roam). The Pathway Prayer Process takes us past the astral plane and directly into the realm of the Akasha. If someone opens the Records using the Pathway Prayer Process and following the Guidelines, they will *not* be going to the astral plane. If someone accesses the Records in a different way, I don't know where they will end up! If your friend has no trust in the system she uses to access the Records, it's wise for her to avoid that system. I have not

had that experience and consistently find the Records to be clear, safe, supportive, kind, respectful, and encouraging.

Q. What is the difference between reading the Akashic Records and mediumship?
A. The distinction with mediumship is simple: A medium works directly with the deceased to conduct the reading. We do not do that in the Records; we ask if the Loved Ones have something to share. Sometimes they do, sometimes not. We have to be flexible. One way we know we're in the Records is that our Loved Ones have the choice to participate or not; we can't force them. And a critical difference is that the Loved Ones are not "doing" the reading. They are never the central authority in any reading; rather they are simply participants of their own volition.

Q. What is the difference between a dream and being in the Records while asleep?
A. There is a critical difference. When in the Records, we are awake, aware, and conscious. We have no authority over our dream states. While dream activity may certainly intersect and overlap with the Akashic Realm, it is not the domain of the Akasha. We don't have any conscious authority over any state when asleep. While we may collide with the Records when asleep, we don't really engage, and because we have no authority from this position, we can't be productive. It's as if we are observers on a bus traveling through the Akashic neighborhood, unable to get off the bus and connect with the inhabitants. It may catch our fancy, but it's not enriching in a meaningful way.

Q. Can I change the words of the Prayer?
A. I have come to understand that the Pathway Prayer is like a GPS for the Heart of the Akashic Realm. If the words are changed, it's like taking a different road. You may end up in

the Akashic Realm, but you may not be in the Heart of the Akashic Records. Think of the Grand Canyon. If you take one road, you end up on the North Rim, another road takes you to the South Rim, a boat could bring you in via the Colorado River, or a mule can take you to different elevations. If you decide to change the words of the Prayer for any reason, please understand that the corresponding curriculum in this book will be flat. It's not helpful to try to force any other method into this body of work.

DIFFERENT USES FOR THE AKASHIC RECORDS

Q. Can we open the Records of a deceased loved one?
A. People often want to open the Records of their deceased loved ones, and in those cases, I graciously decline. The deceased are not in an ordinary state of consciousness, and are unable to request a reading, which is why we do not read them. But it is totally appropriate to open the Records of a (living) son and ask about his relationship with his mother. He has the consciousness to receive the communication, so that's the best route. I make no promises, but sometimes the deceased surface to comfort those left behind. We always offer the requester the reading.

Q. Is there a way to clear space while in the Records of an address? What kinds of questions should my client ask while in the Records of their home to make changes to its energy?
A. Space clearing is treated much the same as working with others. First, it's wise to do a reading on the owner and address their issues with their Records open. Find out what they want for their home/space. Ask to be led. Every situation is a bit different, but generally speaking, look for the exact nature of the problem, the point of origin, and how this difficulty

has been supportive to the people involved. Then, close the Records of the person. This often does the trick. If not, with the permission of the owner, open the Records of the place. Ask the same questions. This should cause the shift they seek.

Q. What is the role of angels in the Records?
A. Angels do not have authority in the Akasha. Angels are known for their individual identities, whereas the Masters, Teachers, and Loved Ones work in groups.

Q. What is the role of spirit guides in the Records?
A. Much like angels, spirit guides are known for their personalities and implements. Whereas in the Records, our Masters, Teachers, and Loved Ones work in groups, conveying a group consciousness to us, along with not being available to us individually.

Q. Who determines when someone gets a reading?
A. It is a sacred privilege of each person to decide if and when they get an Akashic Record reading. Some of us have lived many lifetimes with no desire to have a reading. Others have scores of sessions in one incarnation or another. What is most significant is that it is up to every person to determine the perfect time, place, and reader for them. We never insist that another has a reading. It is not for us to say; it is for them. We only open the Records of another person who is at least eighteen years old and with their express permission. They must be able to ask, one ordinary human to another, for a consultation.

Q. Who manages the Akashic flow of energy?
A. I like to think of the Records as a body of energy, perhaps like electricity at the source. Akashic Energy is intended to be useful for us rather than overwhelming. This is where the

Lords of the Akasha come into the picture, as they maintain the purity of the energy and direct the flow so we can make positive use of it in our human experiences. Without the Lords adjusting the flow, the energy would just spill all over us and not be useful. With the Lords of the Records at the helm, they direct the flow in ways that are useful for us. Unbridled energy without direction can be harmful.

Q. Is it possible for me to open someone's Records (with their permission) even while they are not on a live call with me? For example, can I explore someone's Records and then report back to them? Do you recommend email readings?
A. I do not, and I have not offered email readings. Working in the Records through the Pathway Prayer Process for me means meeting with people in real time, connecting in person, on the phone, or on a video call. Go ahead and try doing a reading this way and let us know your results.

Q. How often should we offer readings to a client?
A. I like to leave it up to the client whether or not they want another session. For some, one reading in their whole life is adequate. For others, in times of turbulence and change, they may want a reading monthly for a few months and then not for years. Some people like to have an annual session. It's different with everyone. When working, I like to give them as much as I can deliver. If they want more, they'll call.

READING YOUR OWN RECORDS

Q. There have been a few times when I have become distracted or even dozed off while in the Records. What is the best way to get reconnected?
A. Yes, it happens, especially when we are first learning; we get distracted and slip out of the Records. Don't worry, it's okay. Just go back to the third stanza of the Opening Prayer and read it out loud again. This normally does the trick. If not, close the Records completely and try again at another time. If you are working with another person, take a little break, get some tea or water, and try to reopen the Records from the beginning. Try not to be alarmed when/if this occurs, as it's quite common!

Q. Can I open my Records at the beginning of the day and leave them open until bedtime?
A. It is really distracting and disempowering to try to walk through our everyday life in an altered state. When doing so, neither state is optimal nor ideal. When we are in regular life, it is best to be in an ordinary state of awareness to be effective.

Q. Sometimes I get very detailed responses in the Records, and at other times, they are more general. What do you think?
A. Yes, this happens in the Records. Sometimes we get very specific information and, at other times, nothing at all. We want to stay open-minded to the Records about what comes to us, and it can be different for different questions. Take the wisdom provided and follow it, even if you think you are just "making it up." Check to see if the suggestion is kind, loving, and positive. If it is, you can be pretty certain that the Records are coming through. If it is just plain ridiculous or mean, then it is not the

Records, in which case you may want to reread the Prayer and/or double-check that you are following the Guidelines.

Q. Is it normal to receive answers via automatic writing?
A. If it's beneficial for you to write in your Records, by all means do it! As you progress in your relationship with your Records, it is powerful to explore different ways of receiving—whether silently, writing, or even speaking out loud. I encourage you to try them all. You'll know what is best for you and will learn which means of transmission delivers which type of guidance. As we work in the Records, the Light of the Akasha begins to move through us into our lives.

Q. Am I doing it right? How do I know when I am in the Records?
A. The rule of thumb is if you are getting information that is loving, clear, generous, and open, then you *are* in the Records. If you are getting information that is fearful, negative, and constricting, then you are *not* in the Records. If you have the Records open and want to go deeper to make a stronger connection, you can simply repeat the third stanza of the Opening Prayer. This will take you in a bit deeper.

Q. What happens if I have trouble accessing the Records?
A. The Pathway Prayer Process is a reliable, dependable, and responsible method of accessing the Akashic Records. Students using the Prayer and following the Guidelines are opening the Records. Being able to open the Records does *not* take a lot of practice. Gaining confidence in the information you receive while in the Records *does* take some practice.

Q. Am I really working in the Akashic Records? Because I am getting nothing.

A. Very few people see or hear things when they first start using this method. Most people receive information in the form of knowing, which sounds like your own voice coming from within yourself. When working with a student who is new to the Akashic Records, we check to make sure they are following the protocol and that they are saying the Pathway Prayer correctly. If those two things are correct, then they are in the Akashic Records.

In the energy of the Records, describe what you are seeing, feeling, and hearing. Perhaps introduce yourself to the Masters, Teachers, and Loved Ones. Ask them, "What is the best way for us to communicate?" If it still seems like you are not getting any information, in your normal state, ask a question about an issue you have. Write down anything that occurs to you. Then, open the Akashic Records and ask the same question. Keep practicing, and you will become more confident in perceiving the subtle energy of the Records.

Q. Is the Pathway Prayer copyrighted? Are there any limitations on its use?

A. Yes, the Pathway Prayer Process to Access the Heart of the Akashic Records was copyrighted by me (Linda Howe) in 2001. It may not be altered or reprinted, but it can be used by anyone who is called to this work.

Q. Are there any physical places where we are not supposed to open our Records, like a cemetery or hospital? Can we open our Records in public places, for example, while traveling on a plane?

A. You can open the Records anywhere you like. There's no reason you should not open the Records in public places.

I open my Records all over the place—on airplanes and trains, in churches, libraries, and museums. Just go ahead and say the Prayer—I do it all the time! If it doesn't seem appropriate to say the Prayer out loud in a certain location, then choose someplace more private. I advise you to do whatever feels comfortable for you.

READING THE RECORDS OF OTHERS

Q. Can I read anyone's Records?
A. NEVER OPEN THE AKASHIC RECORDS OF ANYONE WITHOUT THEIR VERBAL REQUEST OR PERMISSION. IF THEY ARE UNABLE (FOR ANY REASON) TO MAKE THE REQUEST OR GRANT PERMISSION, DO NOT OPEN THEIR RECORDS!

I know there are "spiritual" schools that encourage spying, but the Linda Howe Center for Akashic Studies is definitely not one of them. Our work is sacred. In order to be effective, sacred trust is required with the Akasha and the people we serve. Uninvited exploration is akin to psychic abuse and never, ever appropriate.

Q. I am new at this. How do I know if I am any good? I get so nervous and wonder when this will pass.
A. It seems the best way to develop as a practitioner is through practice! You may be extremely talented, but if you don't practice, then you won't improve. If you want to know how you're doing, ask the client. Just ask if the reading was helpful to them in the moment. But don't put a lot of pressure on them to evaluate you. For yourself, notice if you are judging or being critical of the person. If you understand why they have made their life choices, you're in good shape. Be patient with yourself.

Q. A client keeps coming for readings but fails to take the suggestions I give. Must I keep offering them readings?

A. If someone keeps wanting readings and is not applying the suggestions, then the readings become repetitive. The idea is that wisdom is revealed and then the client has to act or integrate it into their life. If they don't, the Records don't bring more wisdom forth. If a client seems stuck or reticent to implement your suggestions, you could suggest a session exploring how to implement the suggestions based on the reality of who the person is. You do not have to keep offering them readings. It can be confusing to follow the Light, but it's the best way. We never want anyone in the chair who does not place themselves there of their own volition.

Q. Can I ever refuse to read the Records for someone?

A. Yes, there are situations in which you can graciously decline the opportunity to open someone's Records. If they are younger than eighteen, they do not ask for a reading, they are drunk or high, they are clearly mentally disconnected, or they are unable to sit still, please say no. And, of course, since people who are deceased or in a coma cannot give permission, you should not read them either. A person must be able to ask and show up for the reading.

That said, it is not up to us to judge their motives. We always have the choice of saying no for any reason; in fact, it's your option as a reader. That said, there is a paradox at work here. On the one hand, you can say no whenever you are uncomfortable with a client for any reason. On the other hand, most people who come to you for readings are having a tough time, are not at their best, and can be difficult. Use your best judgment and trust your intuition.

Q. What if someone is in a coma—are we allowed to open their Records?
A. Absolutely not. You may not open anyone's Records without their express permission. We do not open Records for someone who is in a coma or deceased. Even if you encounter someone's higher self in a meditation, do not open their Records. There are other ways to work with someone in that state.

Q. Two clients each want their Records opened together. Can they be in the same room together? Can I do group reading for more than one person at a time?
A. The answer is no. Akashic Record readings are very intimate and personal. The presence of a third party, no matter how close the person claims to be, is a disruption for the person being read. It becomes a show or some kind of entertainment, then the reading unravels, as the Records do not take kindly to exploitation.

Now, I do know that many clairvoyants and mediums enjoy an audience, but it is inappropriate with the Records. If someone wants to record their reading and share it, that is their choice. However, once that happens, any questions about the content of the reading are between the two of them, and the practitioner is out of the loop. If someone seeking a reading is not able to stand on their own with the practitioner, then they are just not ready to have their Records open, which is totally fine. People can live many lifetimes and not have an Akashic Record consultation.

One of the ways we as practitioners know that our client is "ready" is that they are able to ask, make necessary arrangements, and show up alone. If they cannot perform these steps, it is an indication that it is not appropriate for them to have a reading at this time. We never want to impose a reading on anyone, and we do not want to turn our work into a show.

In rare circumstances, a client who speaks a different language may ask to have a translator present. In such cases, take the question to your own Records first before agreeing to such an arrangement.

Q. What is the difference between describing the image and interpreting the image?
A. Using an example of seeing a deer, describing it would be: "I see a deer. It's standing in a meadow, it's brown, and it seems young. Does that mean anything to you?" Interpreting it would be: "I see the image of a deer, which indicates that you should be gentle with yourself and others." The interpreter should be the person whose Records are being opened and read (not the practitioner).

ENERGY HEALING, PAST LIVES, AND ANCESTRAL PATTERNS

Q. Can I just sit in the Records and be healed?
A. I don't suggest sitting in the Records for personal healing. The most potent work in the Records is active, not passive. Our personal healing via the Akasha is *through* the Records, not *by* the Records. While it is pleasurable to rest in the sacred space of the Records, it is most powerful to engage and be in partnership with them. Explore your personal issues, challenges, and difficulties within the safe space of the Akasha from within the Records to awaken to deeper levels of positive Truths about yourself.

Q. How do we remove energy blocks in the Records? How do we increase the energy level?
A. The best way to resolve energy blocks is to identify them and inquire about their value. We would not have them unless

they were somehow beneficial for us. Our challenge is to comprehend how that is possible! Next, we put our attention on the spiritual perspective. Within the Records, we strive to see and know ourselves and others from the level of the Soul in its perfection. Attention and focus precede energy. As we direct our attention to the essential, Soul-level Truth, the blockages are energetically disempowered and begin to fade away. This is not "magic" but a process, as we grow into awareness of the greatest Truth of our being. It's very exciting.

Increasing our energy levels also relates to the spiritual perspective. In order to unleash the infinite energy within, we have to consider that it is good for us, beneficial for us, to have access to more energy. For many of us, this contradicts our culture and traditional religions, which promote the value and sanctity of unhappiness and suffering as a path of spiritual growth. Yes, the human journey is a land mine of challenges, but our opportunity is to be in the flow of infinite energy and peace, unconditional love, and acceptance, no matter what conditions and circumstances arise.

Q. If we have a current life issue that we believe may stem from an ancestral problem, do we first tell the ancestral story or focus on the current life issue?

A. Always do the reading based on the presenting issue, difficulty, or concern of the client. Ask for guidance as to the true nature of the problem and the point of origin. This will naturally take you to the ancestral roots of an issue. You can take it from there! The reading will flow naturally and be a mix of sharing on the part of the client and the practitioner. The Akashic perspective on people's stories is different from many other schools. I believe that, because the Akashic Records are the archive of human stories, the chronicles of you, there is a real appreciation for the value of the story in the human journey.

And of course, there's no reason to be afraid of people's stories. As you are learning, a story heard is a story transformed.

These questions and answers are from beginning students like you. For more, please see my book, *100+ Questions & Answers About the Akashic Records*.

Reflection Questions for Individuals or Groups

All of the questions presented here are designed to support you on your journey through the learning process presented in this book. They are meant to be answered first on your own and then in a group setting. Working through the questions in these two stages is critical. True spiritual development requires intimate self-examination. Private, personal self-exploration can only be done by you, for you. Doing your inner work on your own strengthens and deepens your relationship with yourself. Even when answering the questions on your own, it is beneficial to be as specific as possible in your responses and give yourself the opportunity to explore your answers.

The second stage involves group interaction with others who are on the same path. Working through the book with a group of like-minded individuals is a powerful way to accelerate your spiritual growth. Sharing your Truths with others who can hear what you're saying propels you forward. Listening validates your journey, connects you with your traveling companions, and expands your awareness and understanding, enriching your experience. Giving through speaking and receiving through listening both help establish a convergence zone for the energy of the Records, which supports the unfolding of every individual in the group—and the group as a whole. Notice your level of comfort with sharing your findings with your reading group. To empower yourself and your book club members, take a chance and share just a bit more than usual. Enjoy yourself!

I. REFLECT UPON YOUR OWN PERSONAL STORY

One of the primary ideas presented in this book is that the Akashic Records hold the blueprint of your perfect self. They contain the story of your spiritual evolution throughout time, including the catalogue of lifetimes you have lived on your journey to discover your ideal self and live as that person in everyday life. Just as the author shares the story of her spiritual journey in this lifetime, reflect upon your own story.

1. What events and occurrences have driven you forward in this life? Do you feel there is a greater purpose in the way your life is unfolding? Why or why not?

2. Do you consider yourself to be "spiritual"? Why or why not? What does it mean to you to be a "spiritual" person?

3. Is there a dominant question for you in this lifetime? Is there one major idea you are striving to reconcile?

4. How is your spiritual journey unfolding as your life progresses?

II. QUEST

The author suggests that you are reading this book because you were called or summoned by an "inner prompting" to find the Akashic Records.

1. Why do you think you were drawn to the Akashic Records? Do you believe there is a divine reason that you are reading this book?

2. What has been happening in your life that made you think it might be your time to learn how to read the Records?

3. What people or circumstances have influenced you to find this book at this time? In what ways have you felt supported by the Universe on this leg of your spiritual journey?

III. YOUR WORK IN THE RECORDS

1. Do you think you have ever been in the Akashic Records just by chance or accident? If so, what happened? What makes you think you were in the Records at that time?

2. Have you worked in the Records through another system like Reiki or hypnosis? What were the results?

3. What do you hope to gain from learning how to read the Akashic Records?

IV. INTUITION AND THE AKASHIC RECORDS

The distinction between intuition and the Akashic Records is important enough that it deserves its own section!

1. In the book, the author explains how intuition is different from the Akashic Records. Does her explanation make sense to you? Why or why not?

2. Do you consider yourself to be intuitive? If so, in what ways? If not, why not?

3. What does it mean to be an "intuitive" person? How do you feel about so-called intuitives? When you think of people you consider to be intuitive, what do you think of them?

4. Have you ever consciously tried to develop your intuition? If so, how? What were the results? If not, why not?

V. THE COMPANY YOU KEEP

The author identifies the critical difference between angels, saints, and spirit guides and the Masters, Teachers, Loved Ones, and Lords of the Records. The first group is made known to the reader by personality and identity, and the second is known by its energy.

1. Are you comfortable with the idea of an energetic being without a specific personality?

2. Is energy real to you? How have you experienced the presence of energy in your life?

3. Do you have a current relationship with angels, saints, and spirit guides?

4. What role does that relationship play in your spiritual life?

VI. A DIFFERENT PERSPECTIVE

The "altitude of consciousness" available in the Records allows a person to view themselves and others from a different perspective.

1. What do you think the author means by "altitude of consciousness"? What do those words mean to you?

2. Have you had the benefit of this type of perspective at other times? Was it helpful to you?

VII. GOD

The author discusses her understanding of God and the Records as a pathway to divine awareness.

1. How do you understand or not understand God? What is your idea of God? What are the key features or traits of the God of your experience?

2. How do you feel about the word "God"? Do you use it in your own life? Why or why not?

3. What do you think about the relationship between spirituality and God, and God beyond religion?

4. Have you had experiences that you would say came about because of God?

5. Does having an understanding of God benefit you in your life? Why or why not?

VIII. ENERGY HEALING

In the section about energy healing in the Akashic Records, the author suggests that there is a distinction between knowing about healing and experiencing healing.

1. How do you define healing?

2. Do you believe that spiritual healing is real? Why or why not?

3. Have you ever had a "healing" session? If so, what did you expect from it? In what ways did your experience match your expectation—or not?

4. Have you ever had a spontaneous healing experience? If so, what about that event was healing for you?

IX. ANCESTRAL RELATIONS

The fundamental assumption of the chapter about ancestral relations is that our relatives are chosen for Soul-level purposes.

1. When you consider your own family in this life, immediate and extended, how do you see your relationship with this group?

2. Can you identify the various ancestral groups to which you belong—including your family of origin, the family you joined through marriage, your spiritual family, and so on? What are the similarities and differences in your relationships with these groups?

3. What are the major themes for you with regard to your ancestors?

4. The author presents the notion of the "black sheep" as a family member whose growth opportunities in this life happen publicly. Their life lessons are obvious and unavoidable, which benefits the individual as well as the rest of the group. Are you the "black sheep" of your family? If so, how has this been for you? If not, who would you consider to be your family's "black sheep," and why?

X. PAST LIVES

An understanding of past lives and reincarnation is integral to the Akashic Records.

1. Do you connect with the idea of past lives? Why or why not? If you do, what is your understanding of reincarnation?

2. The following questions may make it easier for you to recognize the possibility of other lifetimes through your everyday life now:
   - Have you ever met someone and been struck by the sense that you knew them before and have not been able to place the previous meeting?
   - Have you ever visited a new location and been totally at home?
   - Have you ever arrived somewhere and been immediately anxious and urgent to leave for no obvious reason?
   - Have you ever had a fascination with a specific place or time in history or even a historical figure?
   - Is there a place in the world to which you are inexplicably drawn?
   - Is there a place that triggers a negative reaction for no apparent reason?

- Is there a type of furniture, design, art, music, literature, or fashion that you love and relate to for no clear-cut reason?
- Are there people you have a gut response to, whether positive or negative, for no sensible reason?

XI. TIMES OF CHANGE

According to the author, the early part of the twenty-first century is a pivotal time of change in the way we humans understand our divine nature and our relationship to essential essence.

1. Do her ideas about the spiritual journey of humanity ring true for you? If so, how does this apply to you in your life? If not, why not?

2. Do you think that you will continue to use the tool of the Akashic Records as your spiritual evolution continues? Why or why not? If so, how?

3. Do you feel that this is your time of awakening? Why or why not?

4. Are you willing to try "following the Light" in your everyday life?

About the Author

In 1996, Linda Howe set out on her journey as a spiritual pathfinder, the first to provide the world community with a key to unlocking the Akashic Records, a dimension of consciousness containing the vibrational record of everything that every Soul has ever thought, said, and done. This key was her Pathway Prayer Process to Access the Heart of the Records©. A practical visionary, Dr. Howe works with students around the globe to promote applicable spiritual principles and Truths that transform the quality of their everyday lives. Linda was the first to be awarded a Doctor of Spiritual Studies from Emerson Institute. Over the past three decades, she has become a master teacher and award-winning author, doing her part to ignite the Light of awakening spiritual awareness across the globe. She is the author of numerous books, including *The Heart of the Akashic Records Revealed*, *Discover Your Soul's Path Through the Akashic Records*, and *Healing Through the Akashic Records*. For more, visit lindahowe.com.

About Sounds True

Sounds True was founded in 1985 by Tami Simon with a clear mandate: to disseminate spiritual wisdom. Since starting out as a project with one woman and her tape recorder, Sounds True has grown into a mission-driven learning and media company, partnering with many of the leading wisdom teachers and visionaries of our time.

Every Sounds True Book is designed to not only provide information to a reader but to also to embody the quality of a wisdom transmission, unlocking our greatest capacities to love, serve, and uplift others.

Sounds True Books are part of St. Martin's Essentials, an imprint of Macmillan Publishers.